C000195030

Thinking Rich

A man of words and not of deeds
is like a garden full of weeds

Best Wishes

David Shellrey.

Thinking Rich

A personal guide to luxury living

David Shilling

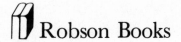

Robson Books

First published in Great Britain in 1986 by Robson Books Ltd.,
Bolsover House, 5-6 Clipstone Street, London W1P 7EB.

Text and illustrations copyright © 1986 David Shilling

British Library Cataloguing in Publication Data

Shilling, David
    David Shilling's guide to luxury living.
    1. Upper classes—Anecdotes, facetiae, satire, etc.
    I. Title
    305.5'234'0207   HT647

    ISBN 0-86051-396-3

Phototypeset by Grainger Photosetting Limited, Southend.

Printed in Great Britain by Redwood Burn Limited, Trowbridge,
Wiltshire.

Bound by WBC Bookbinders Limited, Maesteg.

Dedication

To my mother: who brought me into the world and showed me that from then on it was up to me what I did with it.

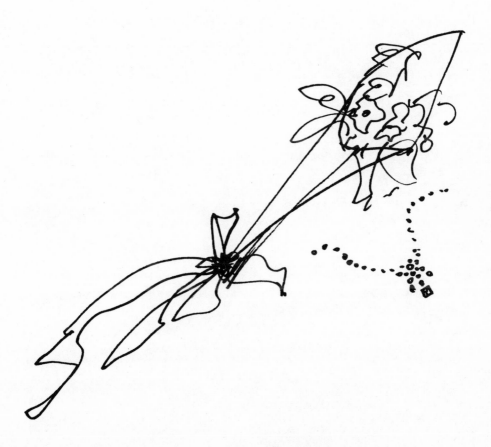

Contents

Introduction

Shakespeare I'm not to be compared with, but Oscar Wilde was far short of the mark when he wrote *The Importance of Being Ernest*. To be a great British writer it helps if your surname begins with the letters SH. What harm did it do Sheridan or Shelley, Shaw or Shaffer? Not being a writer by trade I console myself that with a name like mine I'm assured of the best of company on the library shelves.

As I'm no writer, I set about this book in the same way as I create a collection of hats: I wrote down small ideas, and larger ones, and silly ones and romantic ones – and eventually they all got sorted out. What, you might wonder, do I want to say in a book that I can't with, say, my hats?

Let me start with a story: I was listening to an LBC phone-in, and heard a woman being asked what she would do with a pools win of several hundred thousand pounds. 'I'd buy a David Shilling hat,' she said. The interviewer asked her why she'd buy a hat and her only reply was, 'I didn't say a hat; I said a David Shilling hat.'

If you think about it, money isn't the only way of improving your life, and some of the really good things in life *are* free. It's a matter of priorities: if she'd really wanted a David Shilling hat, it would only have cost her about as much as a dishwasher or a stereo. Rich is an attitude, not a sum of money in your bank account.

Nestling nicely between need and greed is luxury. Luxury begins every day for me when my alarm clock goes off. Well, it is Van Cleef and Arpels in lapis lazuli and gold.

I seldom eat breakfast at home, but often recall a perfect one at Aske Hall when I was a guest of the Marquess and Marchioness of Zetland. (I was in County Durham for the opening of my exhibition at the Bowes Museum.) The dining room, set out traditionally – sparkling silver, fine bone china – is of course splendid, but it's as you contemplate the view that all seems right with the world. From magnificently proportioned windows you see stone balustrades leading your eye to the epitome of an English country-house landscape. Nature's finest greens unfold before you. There is a small lake in the middle, and in the centre of that a small island with a folly. Trees rise up around, framing this tranquil scene to perfection. The garden was landscaped by Capability Brown, but it's Lady Zetland who has brought it into the house with her imaginative use of large plants – even small trees. You may not be able to take your breakfast there, but the house is open to the public.

I'll say it again: rich is an attitude. A tycoon invited nine hundred 'friends' to a dinner and ball at his home in the sun to celebrate a special birthday. He took over entire hotels for them to stay in, and chartered several aeroplanes to fly them all in! *But he charged them for their plane fares.*

I suppose he didn't feel rich enough. It's good to remember that there'll always be someone richer than you – and a great many people poorer.

I started off 1986 feeling rich: breakfast was brought to me in bed on a tray, there was a suggestion of sun through the curtains, and a whole New Year ahead. I'd toasted in the year with Mouton Rothschild 1870 (that's not a misprint) because I was lucky enough to be staying at the unique chateau in Bordeaux. But it wasn't just the fabulous furnishings that made me feel rich, although Mouton is one of the most palatial houses I've stayed in, it was the way I was made to feel welcome all the time I was there.

In fact, it's the thoughtfulness of my hosts that I remember best from all the houses I've stayed in. Whether you've priceless furniture, and amazing butler, valet, housekeeper and cook or not, you don't have to be rich to give your friends a grand welcome.

So why not go and make yourself your favourite drink – a glass of champagne, or tea in your prettiest cup – and sit back and relax while I give you some tips and tell you some tales about luxury living.

D.S.

Champagne

The best way to open it is to hold the *cork* and twist the *bottle*. If it's about to froth over, grab the neck and cover with your hand – the warmth stops the bubbles rising.

Don't be deterred from opening a bottle because you think you won't drink it all. You probably will! Even if you don't, you can keep it fresh for days with a metal stopper available from most wine merchants – or from Asprey's in silver (order by post if you can't get there in person).

My homes

$\mathcal{E}$very home can be a palace – and it needn't be anything like as draughty!

I love doing up houses. Of course I hate the aggravation of builders – who doesn't? Most of those I've known are great at pulling things down, and the only things you're certain they will put up are their estimates – but once you accept this, then your decorating can be fun. (It's even more fun if you can do it without builders!)

This particular passion started when I was a child. I loved changing the look of my bedroom as often as the seasons. I tried to create different atmospheres, moved my bed all round the room and back again. It was an obsession. Even when my parents finally allowed me to have the garish washable wallpaper with line-drawing pastiche views of Venice in colours that you'd never find in anything Italian other than a north-London deli, three months later I'd still got the paint pot out and covered it all over. My parents noticed, of course, but it wasn't so much that they didn't mind as that they realized it was easier to let me keep on changing the room. I think they were unbothered about what colours my walls were so long as our home was relatively clean and – most of it – decorated tastefully. It didn't matter to them what went on in my room. In my teens this redecoration slowed down. I had a more strenuous work schedule at school. I never played around with pop idol posters or film star fantasies, and any decorating I went in for by then concentrated on the body. I'd become clothes-crazy.

The first place I did up was a basement flat I bought in Belgravia's Sloane Street. I'd searched ages for the 'perfect' place to live. There was no heart-rending scene as I left home: my parents were glad to see me going independent, although the flat was far from perfect. But whether it's fashion or interior decoration, I believe the time/money principle applies. If you haven't got the money, you *must* take the time. I have this theory that the more money people have to spend on their appearance or their home then – in general – the less time they've got on their hands (and vice versa). And so instead of being jealous because you can't afford to rush to Bond Street or Savile Row to buy a dress or suit, be thankful you don't have to! Try and find the time to spend a little more thought on your appearance; and with enough time, most people can still look good, whatever their budget.

11

For that first flat I spent my budget carefully. My first priority was to spend money with builders, because I'd bought a flat with lots of 'potential' – which means, even though it was in Sloane Street, it was derelict. I needed to put in a kitchen, which I did in the tiniest possible space. I had French windows knocked into an outside wall – they opened on to just enough yard to make a patio. The room opening on to the patio became the dining room, with cane furniture I'd bought here and there because it was cheap. Some corners can't be easily cut round. Fitted carpets cost a lot. Really good lined curtains cost a lot. I kept the green carpet that was left behind (why is carpet that's left behind so often green?) and with a couple of huge bamboo sunshades indoors, I made what was supposed to be an outside/inside room.

The bathroom I left as it was, except that I used pieces of old mannequins to quite startling effect. A hand sprang out of the wall above the bath for a soap dish, while a half mannequin placed as a kind of chairback and a hand dangling at the end of the chain meant going to the loo became quite an experience, particularly for first-time guests!

I chose the smaller of the other two rooms as a bedroom, and there was space for not much else besides the huge second-hand bed I'd bought (I had to buy a new mattress). The bedroom walls were dreadful, so my solution was to buy cheap fabric and drape it all around the walls and tent it in the middle of the ceiling, with a light hanging from the centre. When you use fabric in what appears to be great volume, you can use very cheap fabric and it still looks luxurious and gives a dramatic effect. (Curtains are so expensive if you can't make them – use masses of fabric and literally pin it into place. I have – it works.)

The drawing room was quite another problem. It was 25 feet square and beautifully proportioned, with bay windows. I went very slowly with its decoration because I didn't have a lot of time or money, and I wanted to get it right. So the dining room and the patio became the main living space at first. I added to the drawing room one piece at a time as and when I could. One evening, I remember, Sir Michael Duff, (who was Lord Lieutenant of Wales) came over from his flat in Cadogan Square for a drink. As he sat down on the chaise longue I warned him it was about to be taken away to be re-covered. He thought I was joking, but five minutes later two workmen arrived for it; so he insisted on being carried across the room, maharajah-style, to the front door. Next time, drinks were in *his* drawing room!

When I was moving to my next flat, because it was the wrong style and didn't fit in, I gave the chaise longue to Patrick Procktor, who still has it. (It was on this piece of furniture that he painted Jill Bennett in one of his more famous portraits.) I find it very hard to sell objects I've discovered and it's an odd pleasure to be able to enjoy the piece and sit on it even though it's no longer mine.

At times, the drawing room had only one settee and a few cheap chairs from a junk shop while I slowly furnished it. But I was fortunate in the classical proportion of the room, and a very impressive fireplace – I could convey atmosphere at night just by using candlelight, placing candles strategically all about the room.

My second home was a three-room flat on Portland Place, in a Thirties block that had just been renovated. The walls had been replastered and were in perfect condition. There was a brand-new kitchen, full of fitted cupboards. It only needed curtains at the windows to complete it.

I set about decorating this flat in the correct way. First I made scale drawings of each room, and of the furniture I wanted there – though even with the most careful planning accidents do occur! How was I to know when I bought a glorious Chippendale bow-fronted settee for this second flat that because of the bow towards the middle of the settee it would be impossible for the removal men to get it through the front door? I'd measured it, and knew it would look great in the living room, but we just couldn't get it in. The owner of the very grand antique shop in the Fulham Road came to shout at his men, but eventually he had to admit it wouldn't even be possible to get it through the windows. Reluctantly, he gave me my money back. For the next few months that settee sat in his shop window, daring me to try and get it home again.

In subsequent homes I have often used the windows to get large items of furniture into the house, and am now quite good at telling workmen how to get window frames out of their sockets. If you haven't done it before, it sounds horrifying but it's easier than you may think – and not to do it would have meant not having some of my favourite pieces in my latest home. I like using large pieces in a room and not too many of them, to achieve a dramatic style and uncluttered look. In my second home the pair of sofas were handmade by Harrods and covered in a William Morris print. Either side of them, I had nests of tables in perspex, made for me at a perspex workshop. I made up a glass coffee table from a piece of glass, cut to exactly the size I wanted and bevel-edged; this was supported by two fairly inexpensive stone pedestals purchased at a garden centre. From the garden centre I also used a pedestal and a stone urn which I filled with masses of dried flowers to create an immediate impact in the hall. The flat had a lot of perfect features, the small entrance hall had a coat cupboard that always seemed to have lots of space, no matter how many guests I had or however cold it was. A further hall had the kitchen leading off to the left, a tiled cloakroom with toilet and wash basin for visitors and to the right the living room opened out. The bedroom and en suite bathroom, and second bedroom, were hidden behind a doorway which led off the hall.

I decided to keep the walls magnolia as they had all been newly painted and I kept all the furnishings light and cream, only using dark brown in the bedroom to create a heavier look and a more practical one! In the bedroom I had brown silk, floor-length curtains and the same silk was used for the valance of my mink bedspread. (I might add that I hate curtains which are not at least down to the floor!) A pair of Chippendale pedestals in deep mahogany guarded the bed, useful for bedside reading, and large lamps were placed on top. Apart from the marble-topped console table on the wall opposite the bed, and a complete wall of fitted cupboards and a chair for leaving clothes on when dressing and undressing, there was no other furniture in this bedroom. I do like bedrooms to be just that, rooms where the bed is all-important. What's important about decoration in some rooms is what is not there: for instance, in my drawing room, you won't find a television, telephone, or stereo – nothing that makes a noise. Bathrooms are for the clutter of everyday life. For a couple a dressing-room for him, a bathroom all her own, seems a luxury you should make a priority. Marriages have been broken over the bathroom sink. Fitted cupboards are a luxury a lot of us are beginning to take for granted, and you can never have too much cupboard space throughout your home.

My next move was to 13 rooms above the shop! Space indeed! When I used to tell people I lived above the shop they usually remained very unimpressed, especially those acquaintances who knew I'd moved from the luxury of my flat in Portland Place. What I didn't tell them was that in one double drawing room we could seat a hundred on gilt chairs for my fashion shows, and still have room for the models to parade down the centre, and then give everyone lunch in another drawing room upstairs.

I remember when we used to have the shows there, I would rush off to Covent Garden in the morning and come back with boxes and boxes of plants to decorate the room, and flowers to wind around the bannister rails (sometimes I placed grapes and fruit as well as flowers around then, which does seem decadent now, when so many haven't enough to eat). Sometimes I bought small trees; in spring we'd have flowering cherries or even rose bushes.

The flat was so large that I had to build two kitchens, because my most formal drawing room was so far away from my bedroom – and I wanted to be able to have occasional snacks in both. In fact the flat was so vast I never completely furnished all 13 rooms. Not only was it terribly expensive, but when you go shopping it's not easy to carry 13 pairs of doorknobs home in one go! I'd arrive back home with a pair of chairs, a table and a cupboard, and maybe not see them again for a month if I didn't use that room again. One or two rooms I did finish quickly, for the rest it was great going around antique stalls, shops and markets. I could collect almost everything I fancied, there'd always be one little corner or other to put it (if my maths are right there must have been 52 little corners and that doesn't include the stairways – 5 flights in all). It is amazing I ever bothered to go on holiday, living alone with a choice of that many rooms to be in.

Interior decoration

The most important decision you have to make when decorating is whether you want a very modern look or a more traditional home. Nowadays good fashionable interiors seem to fall into two looks: either the return to the traditional, with a touch of romance, or the very modern 1980s update of the Italian look that has been around since even before the late Fifties/early Sixties, using white and black with lots of chrome or brass or with splashes of bright colours. Usually this looks best in big spaces.

When I say you have to decide – you may have less freedom of choice than you think.

I particularly hate Victorian houses 'modernized' in the Fifties, and brand-new flats posing as Georgian! It is useless to try to fight the architecture with your decor. Why give yourself the headache of trying to make a charming cottage look huge and modern? It will be much easier to work on getting the best marriage of architecture and decoration, and this will probably give more pleasure to you and your guests.

When you are house-hunting, unless you intend to throw all your furniture away or to leave it behind, you must keep in mind its suitability. However, if you have simply got a few good antiques, there's no reason why you shouldn't use them in a very modern setting – but they must be few, well-selected, and eventually well-lit.

I can tell you one really effective way to do up a room if you've not got much money, and it's really simple: you just buy white emulsion and paint your home, or one room to start with, entirely white. But you only get a stylish look if every bit of the room is white, so be warned! This is cheap, but there are no half-measures. For a little bit more interest you could toy with textures by using gloss and satin finish paint as well. You should make a white floor too if you don't want to, or can't afford to, buy fitted carpet. Anyway, carpet is almost never white enough – paint your floor and don't worry that it's white, when it's dirty you can just paint it again. And if it's a piano, it might as well be white. That's the only really simple way to do up a home without much thought. Frankly, the more thought that goes into interior design, the better effect you'll achieve. Most people think it's all about walls and furniture, but I'd say it was about colour and shape and scale. Start by making scale drawings of your rooms – if plans are available, do use them; but make sure you check a few measurements

first to see they are correct. Once you've prepared your plan drawing, you cut out some of the essentials to scale – say a sofa shape for the living room, a TV for the rooms where you'd have one, chairs, tables, beds – just enough to give you an idea of the space you've got to play with. If you want to do a quick, rough, job then a pencil and a child's squared notebook will do, but if you get graph paper, a pair of compasses (which will only cost around £2), Snopake for mistakes and good scissors you can be much more precise. This exercise will be worth every moment you spend on it, by helping you to avoid expensive mistakes – and don't think everyone isn't always on a budget when doing up a house! Whether you're doing up a bedsit or you're moving into a £5-million home, there's got to be a budget. Whether it's a Rousseau or a rush mat, there'll come a point where you have to stop and say, 'No, I can't afford that!' Do make time to do your plan; it's not difficult even for people who find drawing a glass of water beyond them. Try and get someone to help – I find having someone to hold the tape measure makes taking the measurements faster, though perhaps the chatter slows us down. But it makes the work seem fun.

Once you've got your plans drawn up, you can think about colours. This doesn't mean you go out and buy paint. *Think* about what you want. While you're perhaps less likely to get tired of muted tones, it will cost you no more to use strong colours. David Hockney's house in Los Angeles is a shrine to strong colours, bright blues, reds and sharp pinks. Some colour schemes in the Brighton Pavilion are far from subtle.

First, decide what objects you are going to put in each room (and always think of just one room at a time). You may want to rearrange later, so put the schemes together and aim at overall harmony. If you haven't got swatches of colours of the furniture you've got to use, why not push it all together in a corner of the room, add in all the ornaments, rugs, and cushions and decide if there's any overall tone or mood? Work towards tying them together in a colour scheme. If you're starting from scratch with no object to place in the room it's easier – and yet how *do* you first decide what colours to start off with?

With paints, I always like to mix my own colours – why be tied to a shade card of a few dozen when there are thousands to choose from? I might add that though I know exactly what I'm looking for each time, my decorators don't necessarily do so. The ceiling in my drawing room had to be repainted eight times until I was happy with the colours, because they didn't think they needed me to mix the very palest of blues that I wanted. Almost white or the palest of blue ceilings in formal rooms will suggest sky, and being at peace with nature. In fact, the room – which appears totally cream – has walls in a sort of banana colour (my own mix of colour: a little pink, a little yellow, on an off-white base). But all the woodwork is white and the ceiling – at last – that very pale blue, with accents of gold along the cornices and outlining the door. I know the theory with buying ready-mixed paints is that you can touch them up, but once a colour is on it fades, and it can be almost impossible to patch up the paint in a room anyhow.

Use shade cards to give ideas, but a room in one colour is usually boring. Think what colours go together well to create the effect you want, and remember that lighter colours are just that. White really does make rooms feel and look bigger but dark colours look rich in large spaces, or for, say, making an intimate dining-room atmosphere.

Don't buy anything till you've collected your colours together on your plan – remember you can be daring with colours you're using less of – and where you can't get hold of swatches of materials, try getting an equivalent on paper. When you've achieved a balance of colours you'll want to live with, *then* you set about putting it all together. If you're on a tight budget, don't go for traditional decoration. Try the more modernist approach. You can still have a few antique pieces around if you want to – but be warned, if you love old things. Nothing is more difficult to fake than antiques – it's better not to try to do 'traditional' on a low budget. All reproductions look just that!

If you've very little money – invest in paint and a roller and brushes. One of my friends came up with a novel way of decorating stylishly – with all the items collected from markets and junkshops. He painted picture frames, tables, chairs with heavy white emulsion and then spotted every surface with close thick black painted dots. It took a bit of time and application, but didn't need skill, and for a little interest here and there he did some surfaces black with white dots. A few green plants looked terrific and gave life to the black and white – you could invest in an old zebra skin rug – or you could find zebra print material to make cushions with. A few strong black and white photos (in his case he had Ingrid Bergman and Lauren Bacall, whom he managed to get to sign some of her most striking images) again in spotted frames completed the dramatic look. If you have no pictures and bare walls, but don't want to hang posters or photos, how about painting dramatic designs on the wall? If you're wiring for wall lights you could even incorporate lights in your scheme. At the simplest, build up a design of a large triangle, a circle and an oblong tube. Choose three dramatic colours to contrast with your wall colour. To get an impression of what you're doing before actually putting paint to wall, do a mock-up. If you're not good at painting, get single sheets of writing paper in the colours you want to use and cut out the shapes you want. Juggle the three shapes together till you get an idea of what you're aiming for. Transfer this scaled-down version. If you don't trust yourself with a brush make a stencil of the shapes you require (if the circle is too difficult try a square instead) and spray the paint on. Using spray cans is more expensive but you're sure of a clean edge and a smooth finish. You could also use spray paint to stipple your walls and give an interesting textured, shaded effect. But if you're really on a budget you'll notice those little car sprays don't cover very far! (There are other finishes you can try – look in magazines and decorating books for ideas such as ragrolling.)

Unless you are a great handyman, avoid the pitfalls of wallpaper hanging. But you can still have patterns on your walls – anyone can make a small stencil! My cream bedroom walls were splattered with gold and then a stencil of tiny gold stars applied all over. You can get paper to make stencils from art shops; you can use a spray can which is more expensive but cleaner than a brush (but limits the colours you can use). Your stencil can be as large or as small as you like. A few ideas might be confetti (after all, you can apply as many different colours to your walls as you like, one at a time and be careful of the effects of overlap), falling leaves, or the less artistic could make use of real leaves, stars or snowflake-type shapes, bows. You can use as few prints as you feel looks nice or clutter the wall till you have the effect of a busy wall covering. A wall of polka dots, even, in different sizes could be dazzling.

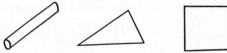

If you enjoy this, you might go on to a mural later. You could always experiment by painting some simple shapes on paper; if that goes well, think big and go for the wall.

A friend of mine in Soho decorated the walls of his kitchen like a large aquarium, with giant fish in quite friendly colours: golds and stripes of black and white, and with wonderful swaying seaweeds in all shades of green. It looked quite normal to see the cooker and fridge at the bottom of all this as if ejected into the Thames. A few lobster pots and fishy accessories put the finishing touch to the look.

One of the latest fashions in decoration seems to be the one for columns, even in 'post-modern' buildings. Classical columns appear everywhere – as plinths for objets such as a neo-classical bust or a vase, or apparently supporting a ceiling! If you've patience and artistic temperament, or a friend who has, you should be able to do some trompe l'oeil columns. Use photographs, or get a book from the library either on neo-classical architecture or on the paintings of people like Alma-Tadema, who draped ladies around bathing pools and included columns galore.

Mirrors always add light to a room, and space. If you find an attractive frame you can always have mirrors cut to size for it. To look really expensive, though, a mirror should be bevel-edged, that means it is cut away around the edge of it. It costs nothing to get a quote for this when you're at the glaziers!

Many people think it is too expensive to mirror a whole wall, or they think only of small mirrored tiles because they're easily available. Mirroring a wall or part of it in one piece can be expensive but it can also transform a room. Use kitchen foil if you need to give yourself an idea of what it could look like, but on the whole I'd leave it to the expert to put it up for you. Look up a glazier in your Yellow Pages, work out approximately what size you need, ask their opinion about quality, and for the price of a phone call you'll know approximately what it would cost, and if it is a large wall what number of pieces you'll have to have.

Wallpapers can be expensive, and to give a clean, smart finish they need to be hung on good flat walls which have been cross-lined with lining paper. Painted walls are easier for hanging pictures, although Walter Annenburg achieved an amazing effect by hanging his Van Gogh on almost tropical-flowered wallpapers at the US Embassy residence in London.

Of course papers can be bought at all prices, and some of the cheap ones are very good, but you can't expect to get the 'individual' look you intended by using a 'mass produced' pattern. On the other hand, at the top end of the market you will be able to order many of the papers in a range (including all my own wallpaper designs) in any colour you want – and many of these will have co-ordinating upholstery fabrics for curtains and chairs, settees and so forth. But just because all the matching bits are available, don't be too tempted – or you'll end up with a hotel-type room, and rather than looking rich it'll look clinical.

When you're doing a modern room, window curtains don't have to look like curtains anymore. Anyway, an urban landscape seen through the window can be part of the decor, an ever-changing picture on one wall. If you want fabric at the windows, just hang a length around the frame and leave a few feet spilling on to the floor at one side. People used to drape shawls over furniture, though now good antique shawls are probably too rare and expensive to use in this way. But you could drape fabric over a chair or settee, rather than going to the expense of 'recovering' in the traditional way – and leave a corner ostentatiously spilling on to the floor. In my shop I've draped fabric (David Shilling, of course) over a rather dull low table and made a huge knot to hang on

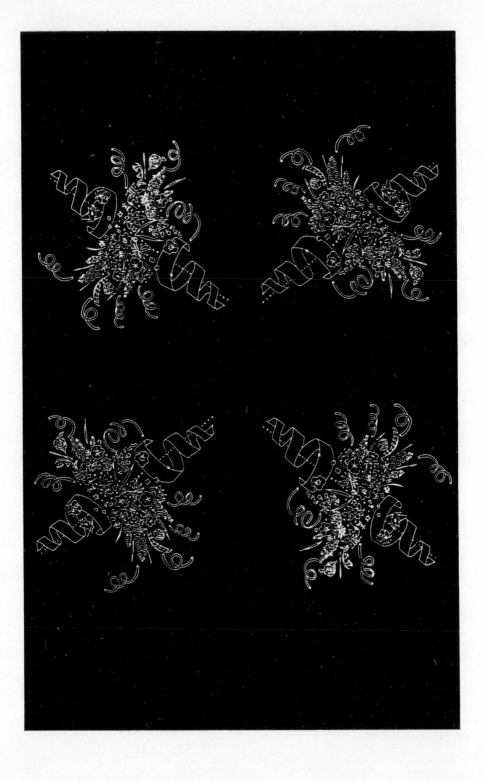

the floor at one corner. Of course it'll get dirty – but only costs a couple of pounds to dry clean and if I want I can always use the fabric length for something else another time.

When I moved into my present home I had wonderful silk curtains made for the drawing room, so splendid that whenever they've been shown in a magazine or on television people come up to me and mention them. Recently, at a wedding, a woman told me she had seen them and now she had 'my curtains' in her house. I wished she'd offered me a design fee, especially when I learned later that the house was a £2-million one near Regent's Park.

When it came to curtaining the dining room I couldn't find exactly the fabric I wanted to have made up, and I panicked as a party date approached. I had an ornate pair of curtain tie-backs, and a couple of lengths of material that more or less went together; but I certainly wasn't keen enough to send them off to be made up, curtain making is so expensive (and would have taken too long). Instead I got some pins and draped the material to look like curtains as a temporary measure. Two years later they're still there. Occasionally I check the pins and one day I'll get round to finding the right material! (Of course I can't draw them open, but as the dining room is on the ground floor I don't mind.)

Window curtains make huge statements of colour and drapes, but doors are still mostly neglected. You can make much of the entrance into a room – after all it should be that and not just a draught-excluder in winter, and something to cut down the noise from the rest of the house. You can disguise a door so that when it is shut it blends into the walls; if you like the idea of having your door in a wall of book shelves, why not? You could arrange a trompe l'oeil curtain around it. Or add decoration like a carved pelmet above the door frame, or if the room is tall enough add a shelf above and place interesting ornaments on it. If you're really stuck for space you could, with taste, put an attractive small, narrow cupboard above the door, but make sure it is terribly secure (as with the ornaments, remember all the door slamming that goes on!) You could certainly pick out the architraving in a different colour, and use stencil around the frame. For an amusing look in a kitchen, say, you could get an artist friend to paint a figure looking through one of the door panels at you – perhaps of a friend or child (you could use a photograph blown up to the appropriate size).

Lighting is one of the main tools of interior decoration. Think of painting with light: open up a corner here, decide to emphasize a table or desk there. You can create mood and drama, warmth and cooler areas within a room by the use of light and shade.

Use several points of light rather than one massive one. If you have plants or screens, try putting 'up-lighters' behind them – these needn't be expensive fitments, since they're not going to be seen. You can use lighted candles to experiment with as you decide how many lamps to use and where to place them.

When you're on a tight budget, a lot of strategically-placed candles or nightlights can give a wonderful look to any space, especially if the walls are white and you play up the feeling of space and emptiness rather than trying to hide it. To give a Japanese feeling to your room, float candles in simple glasses (those given away at petrol stations will do), float flower-heads in other glasses and scatter cushions about.

Try grouping candlesticks of different heights and types together. Once they're lit, the overall effect could be sensational – and if you don't like it, just rearrange till you do. Friends who smoke will find them useful (candles are said to get rid of cigarette smoke), but their biggest advantage is the flattering light they give. Your paler friends will adore visiting you!

Dimmer switches may seem expensive, but I find that bulbs used with one turned down low last an awfully long time, as well as giving a range of light from one source. Living on my own, having a light on here and there makes the house feel occupied – dimmer switches allow me to do this more economically.

When you've done your decorating you can always use splashes of colour from lamps and lampshades, cushions, plants and flowers, magazines – the covers of design-oriented magazines like *World of Interiors* and *House & Garden* usually have strong colour themes that you can choose to complement your own. Ornaments nowadays needn't just be silver and china pieces. You can achieve good effects with marbles, painted eggs, shells, odd objects in glass, ball bearings, nuts, pot-pourri. If you've space, take a cheap circular table, cover with a circular festive cloth – or one cloth on top of another – and group little collections on top. You could have a lampshade made in matching material, even cover a blank book with material (just glue it on) to make a visitors' book. I've seen a wall of a house set aside for the signatures of guests: this might appear to be an easy way to decoration, but unless your friends are literary you aren't likely to be very successful with it – and could end up with something very vulgar! A painter friend did have a wall which he started painting lots of leaves and just a few flowers on, and then friends like Hockney, Beaton, Ossie Clark etc, added the rest – but are your friends up to the challenge?

Having a beautiful home isn't just a matter of the smartest address you can afford, filled with lovely things. It may require you to make sacrifices in your lifestyle you're not prepared for. You can't leave orange-peel on the floor, or make-up on a drawing-room chair.

Nowhere is this more apparent than in the hall, often one of the most neglected areas in a home, considering it's the first 'room' your visitors will see. It is also seen by the gas man and the milkman, so you may not want it to be too exotic, but it should be uncluttered and make an easy thoroughfare through the house. If you haven't a dining room you may think of having a dining area in your hallway, if it is big enough; you could perhaps use a gateleg or drop-leaf table. It's always nice to have a mirror in the hall so you and your guests can check hair and clothes on the way in – and out. You should also have a shelf, if not a table, to leave keys or letters to post close by the door. You should have a safety flap over your letter box, a strong chain and a spyhole in the front door, and not only strong locks but a strong door itself. It would be nice to have a little porch for your guest to stand under – especially if you're the type who is always on the telephone when the door bell rings. After all, this is Britain and it's probably raining too! When you've finally opened that door, the hall should give an indication of the look of the rest of the house.

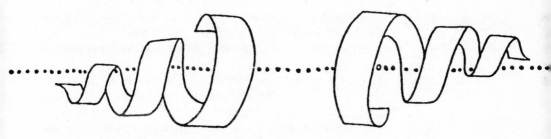

Wallpaper

David Shilling 1985

The best things in the house aren't free, but little matters of style are.

If you've a separate room for the television, you could call it the library – even if the only things to read in there are magazines.

If you want to create a particular impression, with a bit of forethought and time spent with Yellow Pages, you should be able to hire anything from an Antique Bath to a Zebra skin.

Another addition you can make to your home without incurring any expense is a ghost. Of course, while there are those (not me) who really do believe in them and claim to have seen one, there's absolutely nothing to stop you having one in your home. After all, some of the smartest addresses have one, or more.

If your house comes with a history of ghosts, so much the better. Otherwise, dream one up out of thin air. If it's a modern building, it probably stands on the site of something else – the ghost must come from the convent or rectory that was there in days of yore.

When unwanted guests turn up with no warning, you just say, 'I'm so sorry, but I don't think you'd better come in – the ghost's playing up.' And if that doesn't freeze them out, you can keep them out of a particular room (or explain its untidiness) with a gentle smile and, 'The ghost, you know.'

A ghost will be a great conversation piece at a party; and when you get caught out elaborating your story inconsistently you can always say, 'Oh! That one's gone. Our new ghost's much more interesting.'

This is all wonderful until you start seeing the ghost yourself. That could be dangerous. You won't need an exorcist – you'll need a doctor.

Flowers

I love flowers: you put a vase or a flowering plant in the hall, and it makes an instant impression. Just three or four blooms in a room will make the house appear full of freshness and colour, and won't cost you more than one bunch of flowers. (It's getting a bit better now, but in England the attitude seems to persist that flowers must be bought in bunches of ten or twelve of the same – in France you can buy a couple of this, and one of that, and so achieve more variety.)

You don't even need a vase: old decanters, without their stoppers, turn up in junk shops quite cheaply. I quite often use containers of this kind for single stems of, say, tulips in spring or roses later on. I prefer it if I can get hold of garden roses – they have a charm that the bought ones just haven't got – and people with extensive gardens are usually delighted to give away a few; just as they're happy to give away their fruit in season to those willing to pick it themselves.

If you've got green fingers grow plants; if you haven't, use dried flowers. The fashion editor of *Harpers & Queen* was particularly struck by an arrangement I'd done and what she called the 'clever' way I'd used weeds!

My favourite way of using flowers is to choose a colour scheme to complement the room, then in one vase mix as large a variety of shapes and sizes as I can. Foliage is useful both to make the flowers go further, and to give shape and strength to an arrangement. Don't give up because you've had no formal training in flower arranging: the reason for having flowers in the home is to enjoy their beauty, and experimentation will teach you a lot. Though it must be said that some flower arranging classes are very exciting, giving ideas on using unusual or unexpected things with the flowers. Not to everyone's taste – when Lloyd Grosman went round my house for TV-am, he was quite scathing about the dinner table arrangement, which included blackcurrants on twigs. I felt it was creative use of what was available.

For very special events, be imaginative. For one party, my balconies were ornamented with fake bay-tree shaped 'trees' made up of pale pink carnations and roses; I've lined the dining room walls with branches hung with flowers; and used whole branches of cherry blossom in such quantities that they almost recreated the trees themselves. (I suppose it's obvious I don't have to do the hoovering.)

Putting lights into table decorations is also very effective. Tiny white fairy lights give life to a rust and gold arrangement, for instance; this bit of tongue-in-cheek chic sounds nastier than it looks.

Flowers in America are, like everything, taken to further extremes. And there's a shop in Santa Monica that advertises a hundred roses for $19.95 (around £15); good value, but I've yet to decide who deserves such a bouquet.

When I visited a home in Los Angeles the afternoon before a dinner party, ten or twelve workmen were scuttling round the garden with buckets of earth, though I couldn't work out if they were digging things up to decorate the house, or bringing them through the house to achieve instant garden glamour! The next evening, the chrome, black and white dining room was decorated with white flowers, and the garden looked sensational. There were so many flowers inside and out, and one guest failed to notice the Japanese-style ornamental pool in time and went headfirst in.

The best flowers of all are those bought for you. I remember hearing an interview with Brigitte Bardot in which she claimed she married Gunther Sachs because of the flowers he'd sent her. She could easily have afforded them herself (she was a star, she had the white Rolls Royce to prove it), but he literally showered her with roses – dropped by helicopter!

Dried flowers are not always easy to buy, and can cost a lot. Why not try doing it yourself? Late summer is the best time. Take off most of the foliage and tie them into small bunches – then either hang them up or stand them in a well-ventilated dry place (an airing cupboard or under the stairs is ideal, but anywhere will do). You may feel it looks eccentric, if charming, to have them hanging up – if you leave them standing, they will tend to dry crooked. However, if you do stand them, leave an inch, or less, water in the container – it will soon dry out. Hydrangeas, of which I've masses in my house, love this. You can even dry roses (but I think they're a little sad). As you're picking, remember you are not looking for colour but for variety of shapes and textures.

If you want flowers indoors, and find them too expensive, take cuttings from your friends' plants and fill your rooms with greenery and colour that way. Most gardeners will be flattered and offer supportive advice.

Smells

When we think about the luxury of smell, we think instantly of terribly expensive designer perfumes but forget the wonderful variety of smells we can enjoy if not free, then for relatively little. If you are depressed, plan an outing just to sniff the sea. You know it doesn't matter if the sea's out or not – all that ozone's bound to do you good.

It's quite obvious smells do affect our lives. I hate going into a place where the pong of cooking lingers unpleasantly, but just the subtle whiff of fresh food makes a house into a home.

I like to have bowls of pot-pourri around, and I add to their aromatic qualities with a few drops of oil – I'm using at the moment one called 'Fleur de la passion' parfum d'ambience from Paris. Anyone can try to make their own pot-pourri – or buy some, and add some petals occasionally when your flowers have dropped. (There I go again, never throwing anything away!). To revive the smell, turn your pot-pourri over occasionally.

Eucalyptus leaves are good to look at and smell lovely, especially when snapped (only a few odd people don't like the smell). I love the smell of a bunch of fresh mint, and buy it not just to use in cooking – at the same time it's cheering up my kitchen!

Don't carry the smell thing too far in your home though, it shouldn't smell like a bordello nor be like the middle of a pine forest. By the way, the only problem with having bowls of pot-pourri is at parties, when the evening's wearing on, the drink's flowing and you're running down on crisps and bits – there's always one guest who tries to eat a mouthful!

Buying antiques

A lot of people are frightened to buy antiques, although they can be no more expensive than 'reproduction' – perhaps they're intimidated by pompous antique shops, or think they'll be ripped off in smaller shops or in markets because of their lack of knowledge. They lack the confidence to back their judgement even when they see something they like, because they think if it's an 'antique' it ought to be an 'investment'. They forget they're buying something to enjoy in the home, perhaps for the rest of their lives – does it matter if it's not quite as old as the stallholder says? If you like it, and can afford it, buy it. (Haggle if you feel brave enough.)

What might give you confidence is to buy at an auction – after all, at least one other person will probably show enough keenness to bid against you. And auctions can be a far less stuffy place than some galleries or shops to view 'Art'. There are four reasons for going to an auction house: simply to enjoy yourself; you might learn something; you might find a bargain; it's a good place to find a wide variety of items for furnishing your home.

The most famous auction houses apart, you may have to dig around for a really 'good' piece, but at least you'll be able to handle (with care and respect) items being offered for sale during 'viewing'. If an auction is in progress it's very exciting to watch. Catalogues, especially colour-illustrated ones, are often quite expensive, but you don't have to buy one to find out estimated prices of items – you just ask a porter. A good part of a morning could be spent trying to guess which items would exceed their reserves or not.

A word of warning though: auctions are not places to find millionaires, even where the paintings are in the £150,000 league ... most private purchasers of this type of piece are likely to get somebody to do their bidding for them, and the reason so many catalogues have full-colour illustrations is that they are sent round the world to gather bids. In the art and antique world in general, many items are sold merely on photographs or colour transparencies. I was once very taken by an oil painting of a lady I saw illustrated in a black and white photograph in a catalogue. She had been painted by an artist whose work I like and admire. I kept trying to get to the viewing, but things kept getting in the way – appointments, meetings, the phone never stopped. In the end, half an hour before the sale, I phoned up a friend at Christie's and asked her to check the authenticity and then use her judgement to buy the painting for me.

When she phoned up and said the painting was good, and now mine, I wasn't surprised! Something uncanny, that I couldn't explain, had drawn me to it. But I must admit I was a little nervous – would I like the lady when I finally saw her in colour? Her description in the catalogue gave few clues as to what I could expect. I looked at my diary that minute, saw I just had half an hour, and decided to jump in my car, a Mini-moke, there and then. Imagine my delight when shown 'my' picture, to find the black and white reproduction did the lady no justice at all. I put the roof of the Mini-moke down and then perhaps a little surprised attendants placed her carefully in the back. Not the way a lot of seventeenth-century masterpieces leave Christie's, but the journey did her no harm! When I got her home I found she fitted perfectly into the drawing room, and the cover of the book she was holding matched perfectly the peach silk settee above which I intended to place her. It was almost too good to be true.

Of course not all auctions feature works of 'Art'. Some auctions offer a huge variety of items for sale – down to a few ill-assorted teaspoons. Don't worry that you'll be forced to buy something because you sneezed at the wrong time, it's not very likely. In fact, if you intend bidding for something in a crowded saleroom, it's as well to warn one of the staff of your intention or you might even find your bid is overlooked. Do make sure you know exactly what it is that you're buying. You may only want one of the items put together in one lot; if you're really keen, don't be put off – you can always resell the rest. But do examine all the pieces you're bidding for – and also look carefully for damage before you buy. If an auction is in progress, don't bid for anything that appears a 'bargain' unless you have examined it previously – it *might* be a bargain, but chances are it's more likely to be damaged or have something wrong with it that isn't immediately noticeable.

I'm sure there are those who can't resist putting their hands up to bid at an auction – a bit like gambling fever, but at least you're not likely to lose *all* your money this way. But if this is you, then stay away 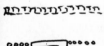 from the actual auction – go to the viewing, and leave bids on anything you really want. You should, in any case, always have in mind an upper limit to what you are prepared to pay. First decide what you'd like to pay, and then find out what the estimate is: some auction houses seem to set their estimates low, presumably to encourage bidders, others high, presumably to make you feel you've got more of a bargain. So remember it's only an indication of a piece's value – don't be too mean with yourself if it's something you really could use and enjoy. (Next year it will be harder to find, and probably more expensive.) The trick, of course, when you're doing your own bidding is sticking to your limit in all the excitement.

detail of settee leg

Auctions are good places to start collections, though if you've an eye for the antiques of tomorrow, they won't have reached even the smaller auctions yet. You'll have to dig round jumble sales and markets. Collections can be made up of anything. There's something fascinating about almost all collecting and groups of objects, and they give you and your visitors much pleasure and enjoyment, even if they don't live up to your financial expectations. Collections can be large or small, they might be hundreds of books, thousands of postcards, or just half a dozen Fabergé eggs. But be warned – all collections start small, but they tend to grow, sometimes alarmingly.

I saw a museum expert on television advising children on their collections and extolling the virtues of collecting Rock memorabilia – picture discs, pop posters, or whatever. The whole interview was centred around what would be most valuable in, say, five years time – which is something no one can know. Sadly, no mention was made that, whether it will be worth more or less, the reason to buy and collect anything is that you should choose things you'll reap enjoyment from. It's very nice if they happen to become worth more money, but the only way to get that money is to sell them – and then you're left without your collection! Remember, too, that fashion can change even in the antique world and values go down sometimes, though not often, before going up again. Unless you want your collection to become your business buy with enjoyment, not gain, in mind (at the moment, if you happen to like typically Fifties and Sixties artefacts, then you probably could achieve both!)

Collecting plates is fun. You don't have to spend a lot – it's surprising what attractive plates you can pick up simply for just a couple of pounds. Display them, either resting against something or you can buy small stands for them, or hang them on your walls in interesting groupings where you haven't got paintings. And, of course, when you get enough you can ask your friends round and actually eat off them! But a friend of mine, whose collection is vast and fabulous, still gets odd looks from her mother who wonders why none of the plates match! You may soon find yourself hooked, and buying some simple guide to help you recognize china 'marks' – you might even make some valuable discoveries, take it up seriously, have a market stall some weekend, or go into the antique business.

In a most basic way first you'll learn to improve your own taste by simply starting to discriminate, and making selections. Automatically you'll decide you prefer one thing rather than another, and soon you'll find you're asking yourself why. You'll start to notice the finer details of painting, and learn what makes one form of manufacture better than another – and often quite accidentally.

Personally, I've learnt most of what I know quite by chance. I remember buying a very pretty little urn in a market. It was in mainly navy blue, on white, with a gold pattern, and I just loved it. It cost £2. I was carrying it home, when a dealer I knew stopped me to say hello. He asked to see what I had, and I took this small urn from its newspaper wrapping. 'Crown Derby, 1805,' he said. 'Didn't you see the D with the crown above?' It had never occurred to me that that was the crown 'D'-erby mark. He added that because of the colour of the mark he knew whenabouts it was made. I felt quite stupid, and had to admit I'd bought it simply because I found it very attractive. I've looked for that mark again since, but not found it. Maybe you'll have more luck. Happy hunting!

Gardens

*J*ust as in your house you have to decide whether you want a modern or a traditional look, so you have to make a decision about the kind of garden you want. There is the traditional garden, where you can choose all the best of British plants with banks of subtly-shaded flowers in a variety of shapes and sizes surrounding a fine lawn, or you can choose a much easier-to-look-after modern alternative, with paving instead of the lawn.

A friend has just had her garden landscaped by Roddy Llewellyn – it was traditional, now it's almost entirely paved, with the area nearest the house for entertaining during the day and evening. A couple of steps lead to another paved area, with a small off-centre pool and discreet fountain. At the far end, where once there was a disused garage, a room has been built – particularly useful for less than perfect days. Once the plants have re-established themselves, I'm sure the garden will be just as glorious to look at as when the lawn was there – but it's much easier to manage.

Whether they're starting a new garden afresh or refurbishing from year to year, many people think only of putting in more flowers, shrubs and trees, when it is most important to landscape and plan even the tiniest plot. First design your overall shape, then fill in with the colour. There are so many things to put in a garden as well as the plants, whether you choose lawn or paving. You could have seating in a secluded spot, or quite central; a few steps leading off a 'patio'; or a folly of a staircase, twisting up with a stone balustrade leading nowhere except towards the sky, and this could either be left unadorned, or entwined with plants, or have pots on the individual steps.

Using water in a garden is not just a matter of fountains and pools, although depending on the scale of these they can be the main attraction of the garden or just an added diversion. Are you going to have lots of plants in your pool, or not? How about a waterfall?

I like the idea of a classical and even slightly overgrown garden, with a full pool and a simple rustic log bridge across. Or you could put logs in your pool to provide 'stepping stones' across, rather than having stone or concrete ones. I also love statues in a garden – if you want a real eighteenth-century effect you can have not just pedestals and urns, interesting wrought-iron seating, and even a small gazebo or summer house, but go the whole way and plant your shrubs in a precise symmetrical pattern in geometric-shaped beds. I believe there is

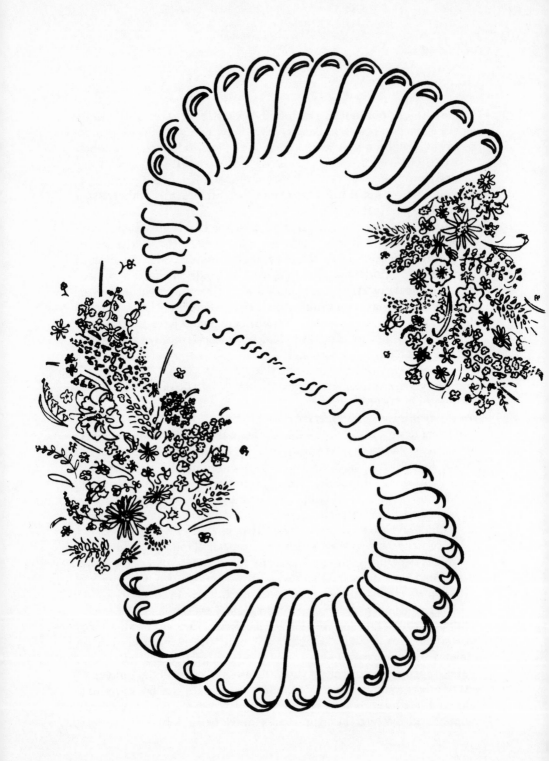

fashion in gardening, as in other areas of life, and arbours and arches seem to be 'in' at the moment and likely to remain so for a while. They needn't just be the traditional way, rustic and rounded, or in thin metal, but can be more modern-looking, made from straight pieces of wood (or stone, concrete or metal) in more modern uncluttered designs. Then you can grow as much or as little around them as you like, whether it is the soft pinks of old English climbing roses, or the searing yellow of laburnum. Choose flowers that you'll enjoy the foliage of the rest of the year when they're not in bloom.

If you're starting a traditional garden from scratch, and you haven't got the two greens (house and 'fingers'), be prepared to be extravagant. Where they say sow every six inches, double or treble the amounts. You can always take the plants out later – there's bound to be somewhere in the garden where something hasn't taken or has dried off. If you don't like something when it has grown, or it simply doesn't fit in with your general scheme as you thought it would, be prepared to take it out. Maybe you've a friend who would give it a good home.

Decide whether you want a riot of colour in your garden, or to create a strong statement of mood around one main colouring, and make a plan of what will be coming out right through the year. Writing it all down will help you spot the lean times.

However small your garden is, don't be disheartened – it can look and feel bigger if you plant it well. You can create not just with plants and trees, but objects and accessories as well. If you want to give an extra feeling of space, a simple way is to put a reflecting surface behind trellis work or you can have a mural painted on your far wall, with a whole extra garden painted on it. You can indulge your fantasies in your garden, if you'll allow them to run riot. How about creating almost hidden areas, which can only be found through small gaps in hedges? Or recreate an arbour with climbing plants for a cool-scented walk on a warm summer's day or night. You could recreate ancient Greece with statuary or build a mini-Versailles!

You can get full enjoyment from the garden at night, too. Lighting outside means you can enjoy going into and looking at the garden in the evening. People spend a fortune on plants for colour by day, and neglect to put in a few spotlights to bring the garden alive at night. If you've an attractive climber on the back of your house, spotlight it.

Even if you know nothing about gardening and you only have a paved patio, you can make it look Spanish or Italian by painting your wall(s) and filling terracotta pots with green plants, especially easy-to-look-after ones with exciting foliage. Don't just think of painting your walls white, try a soft sandy yellow colour for a warmer look.

If you've only a window box or a balcony, you can still make the most of it. For a splash of colour paint your containers. Again, be extravagant with the number and colours of the plants you choose, rather than buying just a few rare and expensive ones, unless you've places to store them year by year when they've finished flowering.

For an instant mini-garden, I've rushed down to Nine Elms, the new Covent Garden by Vauxhall Bridge, and bought masses of primulas – they're inexpensive, come in wonderful colours, and keep flowering for ages with very little attention needed. You have to pay to take a car into the market, where, during the spring and summer, you can buy potted primulas in boxes of a dozen at a time and there is a huge variety of other plants to choose from. You don't have to get there as early in the morning as most people think – arrive between seven and eight and there'll still be a wonderful variety of plants and cut flowers.

There are only a couple of rules: never try to bargain over prices quoted if you're not in the 'business'; and buy in the standard quantity (A box may contain 12 plants, larger pots may come in threes or fours; you may have to buy 24 bunches of some flowers, smaller quantities of rarer species.) If you're not careful, you may find you've spent more money on flowers at Covent Garden than if you'd bought locally, and end up giving lots away to friends! But the place is unique – quieter and less bustling than other European markets – and the choice is almost too great. For Londoners planning a large party on a budget, it's well worth considering going there.

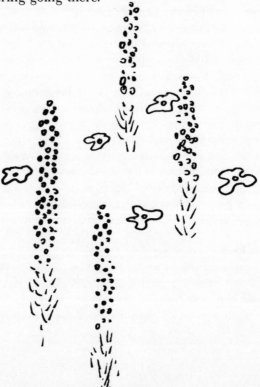

Office working

The place where you work, whether it's an office or a corner of the bedroom, should be clean and relatively tidy – there's a difference between recent clutter that you're using, and things that have hung about for ages waiting for you to get round to them. In some cases, I'd be suspicious if it looked too sparkling clean. On the other hand, if it increases your productivity to have a picture of Robert Redford, or Samantha Fox, selotaped where you can see it do replace it before it goes curly at the edges. Think of it as another version of the wife and kids pictures that appear in fancy frames from GTC or Asprey on 'executive' desks!

Above all your workspace should enable you to do just that – work. Your telephone(s) should be where you can lay your hands on them, with pens handy for jotting down notes – so paper is needed too! I find a large diary invaluable, and I always write down a telephone number with a name when I'm putting dates in! That way, if we have to change arrangements it's very quick and easy to find the number (and sometimes at meetings one forgets to exchange details of phone numbers and addresses). You also should keep only one diary; this avoids slip-ups or inadvertant double bookings – though I know a lot of people use this as an excuse for missing an appointment. 'I'm so sorry, my secretary double booked, I put the date in the wrong diary.'

When you're putting together an 'office' either at home or at work, make sure all the things you need and want are easily to hand – and don't clutter yourself with anything else. Family photographs (the children should be wearing clothes unless they are under six months old) on your desk are very acceptable – but not too many – and not too many photographs of your dogs and cats.

If you want to create an office in your home don't feel you have to go out and buy 'office' furniture. Filing cabinets are great for storage, but they will make a room look clinical and unattractive. Shelves with folders and files arranged either alphabetically, or to a numbered system (with an easy-reference key to the numbers accessible not only to you but also to, say, a secretary or anyone else you want to help you), with the most frequently-used closest to hand, is one of the best systems and much softer on the eye. You can get your folders and files in a good combination of colours too! Just try to make sure you'll be able to get more in the future, to keep a standardized look – or buy at once all you feel you will ever need, and a few more! Each major project I'm working on has a file; when the project is completed, the file is pared down to essentials and put away. General correspondence is kept in date order, and once a year I have a sorting-out session and get rid of what's become irrelevant. I throw it out – this is easier done if there's two of you.

Your briefcase can be your office, and for me it often has to be when I'm travelling. To avoid having to take a heavy address book we write out on fresh sheets important phone numbers, with addresses where appropriate, in cities I'm about to visit. I take two types of visiting cards when I'm travelling – both small, and they fit into little envelopes. One card has my full London business address and telephone number, the other simply has my name on – I add whatever is appropriate, and they seem to make a nice impression. I'll often put slides of my work in the case – I have videos, but the UK system isn't compatible with that used in the States; I always carry at least one pad for sketching or writing notes and more than one felt-tip pen.

I don't carry aspirins or anything like that – I'd never take them anyway – but I like to carry a few crystallized rose petals, and sometimes a packet of biscuits.

A well-organized office should be able to be run by a temporary secretary, with only a couple of minutes explanation. This should include:

How you like the telephone answered. There should always be paper and pens by a working telephone to write down messages immediately – the caller should always be asked if he or she wants the person who is out to call back or not. If a caller leaves a name, it's generally helpful to get a phone number and times when that person can be reached. (To help people taking messages at the other end – you may even be talking to them in a different language – give your full name. It's very irritating to be told 'David' called – David who? Leave a number where you can be reached, or simple details – out to lunch between 1 and 2.30, please ring afternoon; if your schedule is also busy offer to ring back, but leave your number anyhow.)

How to work essential machinery – e.g. electric typewriter, answering machine, dictation machine, word processor.

Where your filing system is and how it works – if it doesn't, now's the time to sort it out.

Where reference books, telephone and address books, essential names and addresses can be found . . . and whether or not you want any of these to be divulged to anyone without your prior consent.

However many staff you have, an automatic coffee-maker makes sense; and there should be an area for all the paraphernalia of minimal catering you may want to do, preferably with a sink. A small 'cocktail

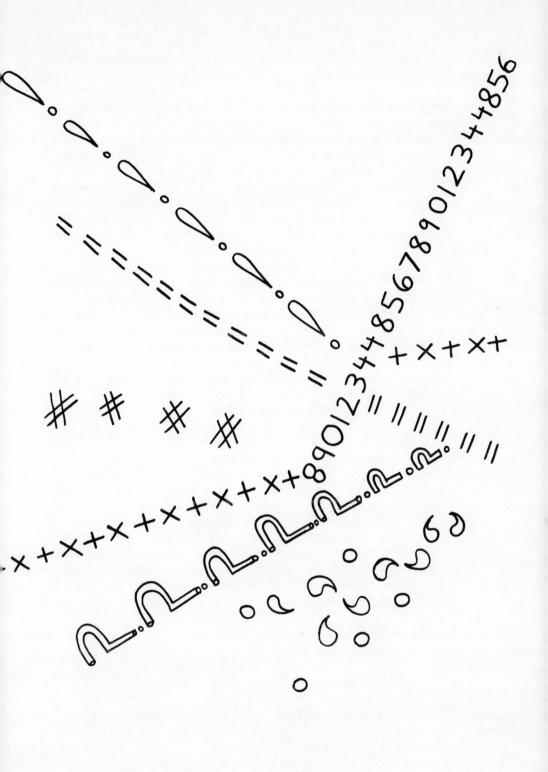

bar'-sized fridge is a good investment if you like fresh orange juice, and to keep milk overnight.

Working lunches: with the trend more and more around the world favouring these in the 'office' rather than in a restaurant, many larger establishments employ at least one person to look after their directors' lunches – quite separate from any canteen facilities they may have.

Looking after a directors' dining room is a full-time job. The advantages of having one are that the directors of an organization get together several times a week; that lunch time is kept to a sensible length; and that the more alcoholically-inclined are kept towards the straight and narrow, if not entirely on it, so more work can be done; a visitor can meet several directors at once.

The same room may be able to be used for meetings outside of say 11.30 to 3.30 (not that the lunches should take that long, but the table's got to be set) and there will be an initial outlay on cooking equipment, even if you have the major facilities such as cooker (a microwave can do, but only for a minute number). You'll need the room to be suitably decorated for meals – wall charts and nude calendars are out!

If, however, you're a smaller outfit, the occasional visitor to a working/office lunch can still be accommodated. You will need china plates, napkins, cutlery, glasses, cups for coffee – and a *clean* table to eat off is better than knees. If you warn your visitor it is 'just' sandwiches, then they're quite acceptable – but offer good sandwiches either bought or made earlier. A salad, or mixture of salads, is an alternative. Have a bottle of mineral water and a bottle of wine – chilled if possible (even standing the bottles in a basin of cold water all morning will help) to drink. The 'meal' should be served on a large plate, and other plates given to your guests: no one wants to take all their sandwiches at once, even if they all have the same ingredients.

If you want to have an important meeting at early morning or at tea time you can offer croissants with jam and butter, and coffee or tea or a simple cake in the ratio of three cakes to two people, six cakes for four so there is a choice and not that awkward decision of whether to take the eclair or the macaroon. You're there to get the decisions of industry going, not take all the time of your meeting with the catering. Biscuits with tea and coffee also add informality to a meeting, where appropriate.

Catering essentials for the office

Kettle, coffee maker, regular supply of fresh milk (can be 'long-life'). Cups, saucers, spoons. A few dinner-size and some smaller plates. Knives and forks. A packet of paper napkins (max. size lasts for ages). Glasses. Corkscrew.

Don't over-entertain people you're working with. One factory I visit always put on a sumptuous long luncheon with cocktails before; there's something like melon for a starter, then as many as six or seven choices of salads with salmon (fresh or smoked) and cold meats, then cheese, fruit and a dessert (maybe a trifle or oranges in brandy), all accompanied by wine or beer, and coffee to conclude. It is all delicious, but not only could they probably get a bit more work out of me if the lunch was shorter, perhaps I could even get an earlier train back! I sit there thinking how I wish they would cut down on this, and add it to my royalties cheque!

Punctuality is important: it's not smart to be late. The hats we produce are no use if they're not ready till the day after the event for which they were ordered. That gives me a discipline, and I'm happy to say we've never let anyone down. (In fact, to guard this reputation, I usually get things ready before they're needed.) If I have a business appointment with someone who turns up late, I find myself wondering if they're taking the meeting seriously. If someone is travelling a long distance, you can't try and cancel a meeting half an hour before it's due; but a phone call to explain any delay is helpful for both parties.

Travel

There's not much luxury left to travel, though the Nile cruises sound wonderful. Paul Jones and his wife Fiona stunned their fellow passengers by having his and hers portable electric fans – by the end of the trip, they were probably the only people enjoying it, kept cool by the fans and their pure silk wardrobe. The moral is the same as the Boy Scouts': 'Be prepared'.

You can't, of course, be prepared for everyone you meet.

Once I was in the restaurant car of a train on the way to Leicester to open an exhibition of my hats at the museum. Arthur Scargill sat next to me. We talked about miners' hats and Ascot, and even Joan Collins! and a little bit of politics. But what I remember most was how terrifyingly attentive the service was. I've never had better service at the Ritz. So many people kept coming up and clapping him on the back and telling him how great they thought he was, that in the end I told him it was for me just like being with Roger Daltrey (I'd been staying with him that weekend). 'You're just like an ageing rock star,' I told him. I'm not sure he minded the comparison.

Air travel is perhaps the most intimidating form. You can't stop, or get off, and for most Brits a flight means either that you're going abroad on business, which is hard work, or for a holiday, which is harder. If you think you might be delayed, travel with some titbits for an emergency: how about a packet of dried fruit or dates? I've even taken sandwiches. If you must drink, it's not worth taking a first-class ticket just for the champagne – take or buy your own. But beware of all the aircraft junk food and all the sugary drinks – travel should broaden the mind, not the behind.

Generally I don't think it's worth travelling first class in the air: the main advantages seem to be the free sleep masks, the footrests and the free booze. Most of your companions will be business people stuck into their company reports and trading projections – not very scintillating. You can take your own mask – one really will allow you to relax, if not actually to sleep – and even your own footrest, if you want to carry it. And it's not good for you to drink alcohol when you're flying; it increases dehydration. What you should drink is water, and plenty of it. The other benefit of higher class travel is that you get more leg room; but if when you book you ask your travel-agent for a seat by one of the exit doors or, failing that, an aisle seat you should be able to stretch your legs out. (In an aisle seat, there's the disadvantage of people passing by; in an inside one, the disadvantage of having to ask to be let out . . . Decide which suits you best.) You'll enjoy travelling more if you feel you've chosen the seat you want.

Good hand luggage is a good investment. The best suitcases are cheap and light. Suites of Louis Vuitton luggage are only wonderful if you've got the staff to match! Leather suitcases are terribly heavy and expensive. Although they should last for years, handling at airports knows no human bounds and it's too sad to see good luggage coming off the carousel all beaten up.

Packing to go away is most people's first travel problem. Of course not all my trips are luxury trips. My favourite holidays have been when Brigitta Appleby lends me Fort Appleby on Gozo. It is a five-bedroom folly on the almost primitive island off Malta, where all I need is T-shirts and shorts. But at other times there's the thought that someone else is likely to be unpacking my case, especially when I'm staying in people's residences rather than hotels. I remember going to the opening of an exhibition of my work in a gallery in Vicenza – a beautiful little town, rich with Palladian influences, between Milan and Venice. What I didn't know when I touched down at Milan airport was that Patrick Procktor had called the gallery owners 'bourgeois', and after going to the opening of his first exhibition refused to return. I arrived on a Sunday night, expecting a light supper.

I had planned my wardrobe for Italy carefully. It was three or four years ago and for the opening itself it seemed appropriate to wear a 'new Romantic' style outfit which I bought at an auction of properties from the Monte Carlo Opera: originally made for *Belle au Bois Dormant*, there was a jacket of cream brocade heavily embroidered with gold, with gold buttons, heavy antique lace and a jabot of lace and heavy lace cuffs on the cream silk shirt. I had planned something equally unusual for the day's press viewings. But I hadn't planned on them arranging a sumptuous black-tie dinner on my arrival. As I sat down on the chair placed under me by a white-gloved liveried servant, in the Palladian dining room, I reflected how lucky I was to be a designer, so that, somewhat like an 'artist', I could get away with anything. Not everyone could have got away with what I'd chosen to wear: a black velvet frock coat (originally intended for Bischitt) embroidered with pink polka dots three inches across. My hosts must have assumed that, as an Englishman and guest of honour, I was entitled to my eccentricity for the outfit went unremarked all night.

However, it's not always my eccentricity that makes a dinner memorable. Visiting the beautiful neo-classical home in Ireland of Lord and Lady Dunleath, I was surprised when our host left the dining table halfway through dinner without explanation. As the guests left the dining room, we were confronted with the vast array of musical instruments which he had set out in the hall. Each guest had to choose one, and provide an improvised musical entertainment – led by the enthusiasm of Lord Dunleath on the organ which graced the staircase.

Plan your packing ahead, don't leave it to the last minute. You'll find you won't take more than you need – and you won't leave any little things out that may be unobtainable at your destination or just timewasting to find.

I'm lucky because I don't always pack my own suitcase. But this means I do have to plan what I intend taking. A couple of weeks before leaving, I designate a part of my cupboard for what I think I'll take with me. This works very well; try to keep together all the things you are likely to be taking in certain sections of your wardrobe: e.g. the right-hand side of your clothes rail for what you think you might take, and keep things you are less certain about taking towards the left. If you're wearing some of these clothes over the next week or so – you're bound to – you'll just have to be careful to see they stay clean or get them cleaned as appropriate... But ask yourself if you absolutely have to wear some essentials right now? Plan to do the packing two nights before you travel, so you have a full day to get any last-minute shopping or dry cleaning done. It's likely to be more expensive and inconvenient to have it done on holiday or in your hotel.

I leave myself two weeks to shop around for anything else I might need. And I take time off to get those things as soon as possible. When my schedule is particularly busy and a trip ahead is likely to make it extra so, then if I don't set aside a couple of hours for shopping several days before I go, I may never get things done at all. Usually if I'm going somewhere hot it's just a few new T-shirts I need and beach things. You should always check the elastic on your old swimwear – and your figure. Two weeks is just the right time to shame yourself into dieting if necessary; I don't use sunbeds, but it's long enough to see results – personally, I don't think you get a particularly attractive tan from them. Have you noticed that you get different depths of tan from different areas of the world, let alone from different sunbeds? That's probably why LA people go in for facelifts so much, because the sun is so fierce on the skin there, and they tan so long. From the South of France the tan is never as deep as, say, an African one. I love to get a light tan on my London roof terrace to top up any tan I've got – I don't get roasted up there too often but it's extraordinary how an hour or two's regular sunshine does keep you healthy looking. And the sun in England just gives you a warm glow. If you're sunbathing here, and have not much time, take your breaks around midday when the sun is at its strongest.

Small plastic containers are useful. I generally have around small shampoo bottles, or similar, into which I can decant just as much shampoo, conditioner or whatever as I think I'll need. There's no point in carrying around a giant bottle and bringing home most of the contents.

It's worth buying small packets of toothpaste, those economy ones are so heavy. Buy a roll of small freezer bags, pack liquid and messy things in individual bags, and then seal the lot up in a further stronger bag (what make-up or toilet bag is waterproof?) You could use a plastic carrier from the supermarket for real economy, and secure the top.

Usually I don't have to buy too much for holidays (but of course it's fun to have a few new things to take on a trip) but what's important for your planned packing is to select from out of your wardrobe what will be really useful, and leave out what is inappropriate. Think outfits at a time, and not just individual pieces of clothing. Then match the outfits to the days and nights you expect to encounter.

Adjust this to the kind of holiday you take. Don't forget the thermals if you're going somewhere cold! A typical check list, for men or women, for a holiday in a warm climate could be:

Shoes – comfortable for walking
Shoes – for formal occasions
White – for sportswear
A suit or dress for formal occasions
Blazer and slacks/skirt and jacket
White slacks or jeans
Several shirts or blouses – at least one formal
T-shirts
Gear for sports intended where rental may be hard
    locally – or expensive
Swimwear
Socks, underwear
Beachbag/case for documents etc.
Toothpaste, toothbrush
Hairbrush/comb/dryer
Soap/towel/flannel
Favourite shampoo
Shaving equipment
Sunglasses
Required medicines or likely requirements
Bath robe/dressing gown/beach robe
Do you need an alarm clock?
Camera and all its equipment

For the beach I wear a digital watch so inexpensive I wouldn't mind losing it - it cost £2.99 in Oxford Street, and its modern black rugged look is so simple you couldn't describe it as cheap and nasty. You need a watch to tell the time to go back home, and to know when to turn over. I feel I can take it off to swim and leave it with my things on the beach, and no one's likely to steal it. Never take more money than you actually need to a beach, and never take valuables - especially not your passport or travel tickets.

I take my favourite sunoil with me (it's Ambre Solaire with coconut), even though you can buy local brands. I once experimented mixing my own oil with bergamot oil - luckily it didn't do me much harm as I didn't get much sun on me that day in London. The results were amazing; I'd never tanned so rapidly. However, according to my hosts, the stains on their lawn took ages to get rid of! I wouldn't try it again. Quite safe, though, if you want to help your hair get streaked in the sun is to apply a little lemon juice (the Gozo house is particularly good for this as it has its own lemon tree in the courtyard) and comb through the hair. You could use limes, but I feel this would be carrying style a little too far!

A couple of years ago I designed for women what I called a suitcase collection (see illustration). It was a minimal amount of clothing all in a distinctive print that gave you a maximum wardrobe for every event. In black and white, red and white, or soft fuchsia on white, the way the items were accessorized would individualize them and, since this was designed to be made to couture standards, there was never that chance of bumping into too many women wearing the same dress! (This happens. I was once at a fashion ball at the Grosvenor House, and while having cocktails I admired the dress worn by actress Frances Tomalty (ex-wife of Sting). It was black, with a striking black pleated fan on one shoulder, and designed by Wim Hemmink. We were waiting for Princess Michael of Kent, and when she arrived we all went into dinner in the ballroom. There amidst the explosion of flashbulbs, it was evident immediately that more than one woman had admired that dress - by the end of the evening I'd counted three others!)

For my suitcase collection, the shoes were also in the print but had leather toes and heels for better wear. The turban was actually made as a hat but if it hadn't been designed by a hatter (you'd expect there to be at least one hat wouldn't you?) you could have wound round your head a long scarf which I'd also include as a sarong for the beach, a shawl at night etc... A good blazer and/or coat, and you've all your needs.

I could design a man's suitcase collection, to cover all occasions, based on black and white, navy and white, or grey and white. A white suit and a dark suit could be interchangeable, a rollneck sweater, couple of plain shirts, pair of shorts, swimtrunks, a casual suit, and/or dinner suit – or a type of dinner suit that has a bit more life teamed with other slacks. For the summer it would be a white silky jacket, which could equally take you to a disco!

One of the odd things about travel is that you can't buy anything abroad and be certain you couldn't have got it more cheaply at home. Quite often, of course, countries export their best products. But I'm sure I'm not the only person who's staggered home with the Nancy Reagan cut-out-and-dress-her-up kit, only to find many London stores had her in stock.

My earliest recollection of doing this was in Deauville, where I bought an ice bucket shaped like a globe, with the map of the world, surmounted by a golden eagle and mounted on a golden base. I can't now think why I wanted this nightmare of kitsch. It was also a nightmare to bring home – the eagle seemed doomed to be broken off, however I packed it. But the biggest nightmare, after taking all this trouble, was to find the same thing available at Fortnum & Mason at two thirds the price.

THE LIGHTER YOUR CASE, THE LIGHTER YOU'LL FEEL.
HAPPY TRAVELLING!

Twenty-four-hour mini-guides

*A*s you travel, you realize how small is the world we live in, and yet how large. I have chosen five of my favourite cities, where you may well find yourself sooner or later, and suggested how you could spend 24 hours getting the full flavour of that city even as a 'visitor'. There are of course great differences, as well as some similarities in each day. These aren't the sort of trips you'll find in any other guide books! These are my own idiosyncratic views, and I hope they'll give you a unique insight into the more fasionable and visual delights of Los Angeles, New York, Paris, Monte Carlo and London.

Los Angeles

It's just dawned on me what it is that is unique about Los Angeles. It's a city that has all the usual things, the same international shops: Gucci, Cartier and Safeways. As usual the toilet paper is not what you're used to, so you wish you'd taken some with you! The hotels are fearfully expensive so you feel like stealing the towels to justify the bill – but they've pre-empted you by supplying them so thick and fluffy you'd need to buy another suitcase to get them away in.

No, the first clue to LA's uniqueness comes in the streets. There's Valley Vista, Rodeo Drive, Beverly Glen, then Chevy Chase Drive and Woodrow Wilson Drive. You should have guessed what I'm referring to from the last two. Here in England we have our odd eccentricities of names, the odd Daisy springs up in a field of Lucys, Sallys and Anns. The titled always got away with using names totally disassociated with their children, and often at variance with the surnames, and then banging two or three together with a hyphen or two. And then if you're lucky enough to inherit a title, you could change name mid-life – start out an 'Honourable', become Lord X, later Earl Y and finally the Duke of Z – but that is a luxury restricted to just a very few.

.But suddenly in Los Angeles my friends' names were Greg and Rayleen, Cri-Cri and Kurt. And it is this that gives Los Angeles its own peculiar flavour. In New York my friends are Nancy and Joan. Here I lunch at Ma Maison with Nanelle and Lois. Jon's best friend is Jaffrey, Greg works with Lori-anne, Roman lives with Nalish. No wonder my Welsh friend Angharad Rees has adapted to life very well with a house with a pool and a guest house! Hers is just as exotic a name as theirs. All this makes surnames quite unnecessary in LA.

51

California is about sun and fun, so we won't go in search of culture on our David Shilling day in Los Angeles. (The Los Angeles County Museum on Wilshire Boulevard is excellent, and well worth a visit, especially for those interested in the history of the cinema – but I'm biassed because the Patrons of Los Angeles County Museum organized a dinner for 120 people in my honour. This makes me very fond of them.) And of course the famous 'Getty' Museum is now open, although it is necessary to telephone to book a parking space – and it is half an hour's drive from the centre of Los Angeles. Some people argue there is no centre to the city – I'd say the best fun comes in Beverly Hills, so to me that is the centre of L.A.

What comes as the greatest shock to anyone visiting L.A. for the first time is how enormous a city it is. And yes, it is essential to drive! People don't walk, not simply through chic but out of sheer necessity. I rather enjoy driving in L.A. because drivers seem less aggressive than in London or New York. You have to drive as if everyone else has the right of way – and pedestrians, the few there are, are to be looked out for! All the top restaurants and hotels, and many stores, have valet parking which (although it may cost a couple of dollars) means you don't have to waste time looking for a safe space to leave your car. You simply hand over your keys and it is parked for you – and it is returned to you when you give them your ticket.

You are what you drive, they say, so if money's no object hire a stretch limo for the day. That in itself is a unique experience. You don't just get a car and chauffeur – a stretch limo looks and feels more as if you're in a small private drawing room. The car seats are arranged to face towards each other and there's plenty of room for six. Apart from the television, there's a drinks bar with press buttons marked G, V, W and W – for gin, vodka, whisky and water. You can't tell which of the two Ws is which till you pour.

You can enjoy all the comforts of home on the move. The latest gimmick to get your business is for hire firms to put book matches and paper serviettes printed with your name in the bar, even if you've only rented your limo to drive to the airport. But if you can drag yourself away from the car I'd say look into the Beverly Hills Hotel, if only to experience the swimming pool. Their Polo Lounge is also an international by-word and meeting place for cocktails.

If your day begins early enough, head for breakfast in the Polo Lounge (breakfast starts around seven o'clock, so you could just come on from the night before!) Don't be surprised that there is an open fire burning in the lobby of the Beverly Hills Hotel, by the way, there always is: it's supposed to give a warm homely feel to the hotel.

If you don't feel like breakfast, or it is later in the morning, head straight for the swimming pool, which is only open to residents of the hotel so you'll have to make friends with someone to get you in. The pool is presided over by the charming and ever efficient Sven.

You'll get your own lounger, towels and side table – I suggest you order a long iced tea (not to be confused with Long Island iced tea, which is fairly lethal at any hour of the day; if you start ordering these for breakfast, watch out! You should be going to A.A. not L.A.!). At the Beverly Hills swimming pool you'll learn more in an hour about the film business – and a bit about rock and roll – than anywhere else in the world. As you laze in the sun – it's not inevitable, it does rain even in Beverly Hills, but more often it's just cloudy, they call it smog – Sven's staff will move your lounger around to face the maximum rays. You are expected to assist them by getting up.

Stars and the megarich hire private cabanas – and hold meetings all day. As everywhere else in L.A., position around the pool is all important. L.A. is unique in the world for placing such importance on your position in restaurants at dinners, public events and places. Restaurants in L.A. are not only 'in' and 'out' but certain parts of the restaurant are more 'in' than others – in some parts it is positively unhealthy to be seen! Only a few New York restaurants are like this; the poolside of the Four Seasons is one of the most notorious. Generally in L.A., the nearer the door you are, the better. Position is taken much more to heart – let us hope you're sitting by the long side of the pool. You'll hear telephones ringing all over and producers winning deals and losing them, though you'd never know it for the word in L.A. is 'enjoy'. The telephones are dotted frequently between sun beds and if there's a call for you you'll hear your name come over a tannoy. You could always arrange to be called by a friend, even start some dreadful rumour about yourself if you really wanted to have fun while you're chatting with your friends. I'm certain that some of the conversations I've heard around that pool are meant to be overheard, and a lot of the paging is just to draw attention – perhaps an overzealous agent at work?

If the sun's out there'll be really 'beautiful' people scattered amongst the tycoons, too, so you may not want to tear yourself away. I'd suggest you have to. Your limo will whisk you off to lunch at the Bistro Garden. There are a couple of wonderful restaurants for people-watching at

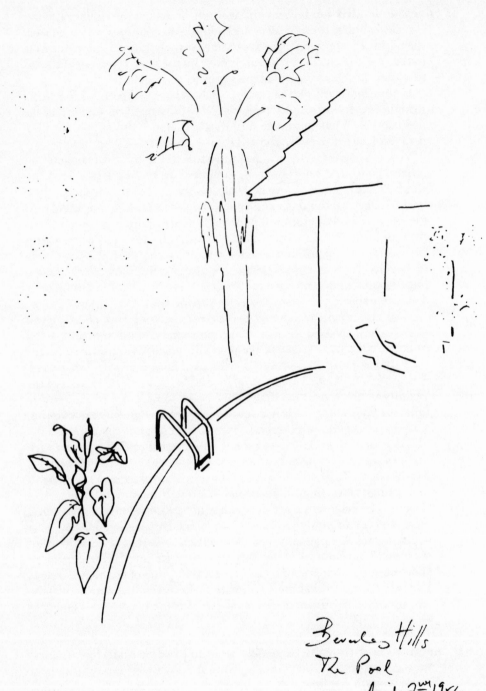

Beverley Hills
The Pool
April 2nd 1976

lunchtime, but the Bistro Garden's location is great for shopping later (here it is chic-er *not* to sit in the garden, the best positions are inside and when you tell people you've been there they're bound to ask where you sat). This restaurant has the advantage of being close to Rodeo Drive. If you own a David Shilling hat, this is one of the places to wear it! Women do occasionally wear hats here and they certainly dress up! Order a daiquiri before your meal, and have a soufflé for desert, but you may find you have to hurry the food along because after all you didn't come here to eat and there's much to see outside.

You can walk to Rodeo Drive, it's only a few hundred yards along Wilshire Boulevard – opposite the Beverly Wilshire Hotel (where there's a small Tiffany's, if you miss the one in New York City) but last time I lunched at the Bistro we didn't even walk that far, but Rolls'd it straight over to Giorgio's, a one-minute journey. This is still an intimate store, though because of the enormous sales of the perfume it has expanded with a larger department for perfume with its own separate entrance. But Giorgio's isn't just the perfume. At the bar in the centre of the store Michel makes probably the best cappuccinos in the whole world. He adds brandy and Kahlua to strong black coffee, tops it with whipped cream and sprinkles it with cinnamon.

As well as clothes for men and women Giorgio's has a huge range of Judith Lieber handbags. They are metal, studded with diamanté, and some of the most expensive and prized handbags in the world, and at $2,000 or more you might think they should be. I've seen them in Beverly Drive sold among antiques and real jewellery. But don't spend too long admiring Giorgio's because the rest of the quite short street has the best of Europe's stores like Chanel, Montana, Fred, Nina Ricci, Van Cleef and Arpels, Cartier, as well as American Lina Lee, Jerry Magnin, David Orgel for silver and china.

Now shopping fever's set in, go to the Beverly Center where parking is easy. If you haven't got the limo, the shops are more affordable here with lots of fun clothes and accessories. By now, if you get to the top floor, you deserve a strawberry coated in milk chocolate at the Ultimate Nut and Candy Store (50 cents each), probably one of the great luxury bargains!

And now it's time to head for Melrose Avenue. Here are the familiar fun shops, more King's Road than designer label, with many antique stores. These are arranged haphazardly but don't expect bargains – there's everything from art deco to huge Sèvres urns and important museum-quality pieces so unpretentiously arranged you may be fooled into asking prices – but here it's more than likely true that if you have to ask a price you probably can't afford it. (There are lots of copies too, watch out especially for very convincing lamps.) Down Melrose you'll find the Pacific Design Center – also called the Blue Whale because that's what the building looks like. It's a huge warehouse for interior designers and, although the public can look round, purchases can only be made through a bona fide interior designer. But it is a great opportunity to see all styles and types of interior treatment all under one roof.

By now it is time for cocktails. From 5.30 the bar at Trump is buzzing. Here is one of the 'in' places for cocktails. The 'pommes frites' are wonderful. And if you'd rather have refreshment than alcohol try club soda with a little lime juice and ice, very refreshing, and drink up because L.A. dinner is early, normally 7 or 8 at the latest, but starting at 6.30 is not that unusual.

You probably know that what an American princess makes best for dinner is... reservations. Yours should probably have been made at Spago, if it's still as trendy as it has been for the last twelve months. L.A. restaurants are in and out very quickly, except for a few classics like Chasens and The Ivy, Jimmy's and Ma Maison whose number is unlisted but is 655 1991. Meals in L.A. usually offer the opportunity to eat kids' style, pizza and hamburgers, fun-food, as well as (depending on the restaurant) the best of French and Italian cuisine. Californians, who of course are very figure-conscious, will probably order just a salad at lunch and they are not likely to eat more than two courses at dinner. Nevertheless portions are normally more than generous, and starters and desserts both very tempting! You may choose pizza at Spago but I prefer the smoked salmon, sour cream and chives pizza at The Ivy. I've never seen that combination anywhere else in the world – yet! I'd say it's the best pizza in this pasta-crazy town.

L.A. isn't a great town for after-dinner nightlife. The reasoning is if you're filming next day you'll probably have to be at the studio at six – and if you're not filming next day you don't want everyone to know it by your being out so late! And if you're in business, the couple of hours' time difference with New York means your telephone day starts at seven.

If you must go dancing the clubs are in and out so quickly you'll have to seek advice. One of the few that stays 'in' is Rainbow on Sunset, and at least it's near Spago and easy to find. The latest ones are hidden away downtown (that's a twenty-minute drive, and you're recommended not to leave your Mercedes unattended if you want to see it ever again) and they come and go with names like Power Tools and Helena's. Someone knows where they are but, like the rest of downtown, you don't have to.

Disneyland is open at night and you could go there, if you can't extend your stay. Really you need to spend some time there in summer.

There are often long queues for the rides, especially the Pirates which is supposed to be the best! I loved it. And you do need a lot of time for the Universal Train so get an early night and plan those two for tomorrow.

Universal Studios give visitors a guided tour around the lot, which is very informative if you've never been to a film set before. But it takes up the best part of a day, for once on the 'train' you can't get off easily. Disneyland is an hour or even longer drive out from the centre of L.A., and if you go with children they'll not want to leave quickly. Why should they, when the price of admission is good for rides all day?

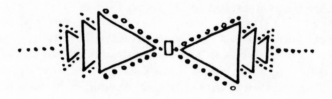

New York

New York is an over-the-top city. The World Trade Center is 1,350 feet high, with 110 floors and the second-tallest building in the world, dwarfing the Empire State Building. New York prices match! New York pace is crazy. From the moment you hear the howling of horns outside your bedroom window early morning (you'd never need an early morning alarm call in New York, the traffic noise seems to rise however high up you are) there's a buzz in the air. Not many people would visit New York for just one day. But during your stay why not try one David Shilling day in one of the most exciting and style-oriented capitals of the world. Of course there is so much else in New York, you'll have to plan your other days to suit. Because the traffic in New York is your greatest enemy, we stay mostly on foot; even a car with a chauffeur is more of a problem than an asset, without a chauffeur it's a nightmare. Other drivers are impossible, they pull out in front, the one-way systems are incomprehensible, the fast roads lead you miles away from where you want to be and only the very central part of Manhattan is easy to understand because of its numbered street system, like a crossword puzzle, you want 57 down and 4 across. When you get downtown to SoHo your taxi drivers are likely to get lost. You'll not even fare much better if you try to get around with a limo – you'll just be more comfortable when you're stuck in a traffic jam.

Start off at the Pierre Hotel. On Central Park, this is not the most lively hotel in New York, but it's where the President would most likely be staying, if he's in New York. And it shares with the Plaza the best location in New York for shopping. The Pierre has the added chic of a Bulgari boutique on the ground floor – surely makers of some of the best modern designer jewellery and their distinctive gold watches, with ribbed gold bracelets, are still hankered after even by the very rich.

Their gold necklaces of chains with ancient Roman-style coins of varying sizes mounted in gold at the centre are worn as status symbols by seriously rich women throughout the world, and they've been widely copied at all price levels. A room at the Pierre would cost from $150 with breakfast, but if you're not starting your day with breakfast in bed you could just take your breakfast like Audrey Hepburn – except in front of Bulgari's window instead of Tiffany's. Look towards Central Park, which simply doesn't compare with our London parks, then make your way up to Madison Avenue, to Bloomingdale's. On your way do your window-shopping. You might indulge in a couple of chocolates at my favourite New York chocolatier Teuscher, and I mean just two. They will be boxed in great style, perhaps as a domino, perhaps with some pretty little spring flowers on top, depending on the season. A single chocolate costs less than a dollar; two of their favourite champagne truffles in a pretty box around four dollars, but if this shocks you be glad you passed by Caviarteria, a shop devoted only to caviar.

On Madison Avenue go from 'Limited', a new store that feels friendly on all five storeys, with video screens in the basement and a great display of young carefree fashion, some surprisingly cheap (I saw T-shirts big enough to wear as dresses at around £10 – in just the right colours), then wander up Madison as far as your legs will carry you – past so many milestone names in fashion that it'd almost be easier to list the few that aren't there; for starters, there's Yves Saint Laurent, Sonia Rykiel, Ungaro, Givenchy; Ralph Lauren's store is more like a townhouse with English antiques; and there are terrific specialist accessory shops which all makes not buying a new wardrobe quite hard. Valentino moved from his Fifth Avenue shop here. For a bit of culture further up the street (the Seventies, as they say in New York) more antique shops and galleries appear, but they're dotted all over between Fifty-ninth and the Eighties.

If you get as far as this you deserve a great Tortle cookie, from My Most Favorite Dessert. All around the city are great food temptations – my friend Doris owns this one and I have a wonderful couple of days when a tin of her quite incredible cookies arrive in London.

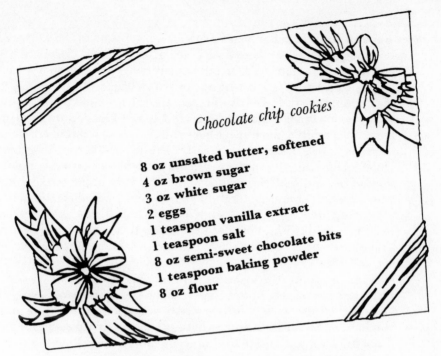

Chocolate chip cookies

8 oz unsalted butter, softened
4 oz brown sugar
3 oz white sugar
2 eggs
1 teaspoon vanilla extract
1 teaspoon salt
8 oz semi-sweet chocolate bits
1 teaspoon baking powder
8 oz flour

Preheat your oven to 350°F, grease a baking sheet. Cream
the butter and sugars, add eggs and vanilla. Sift the dry
ingredients together, and add to the mixture, then add the
chocolate bits. Spoon on to baking sheet in teaspoonfuls.
Bake for 8-10 minutes. The centres should be slightly soft
when you remove the cookies from the oven. Allow them to
cool before removing from the baking sheet. Vary your
cookies by adding nuts or coconut to taste.

The other temptation for me in New York are the Ray's Pizza stores.
    Whatever time you started out, around 11.45 you should be heading
for Bloomingdale's – when you get in the door head straight for the top
floor – the Main Course – and stay on the escalators till you get up
there. If you stray too soon, you'll never make it; meander around the
home department, then take the escalators down and wander as you
will. Don't be surprised that you can buy some quite inexpensive
things, as well as the astronomically priced – and English tea in the
basement! If you really want to buy something in Bloomingdale's you
needn't wander at all. Just tell them what you're looking for and
they'll bring it to you. They have specialist staff who will, for instance,
choose not just the dress for you, but shoes, gloves, hat, jewellery to go
with it, at absolutely no extra charge, of course.
    Leave by 12.30 and head down along Fifty-eighth Street to Park
Avenue, doing a bit more window-shopping en route.

'**You have to have lunch** to make plans for dinner,' says my friend Soraya Khashoggi. Pop into Harry's Bar for a light lunch. Certainly here you're likely to find the rich and famous doing just that in a frenetic setting. Have a Bellini to cool you and calm you, and if it's Friday try their special fish dish. Desserts are sensational, huge meringues topped with cream, other Italian-style confections, all loaded on to a tiny table. (There isn't much space here and the whole atmosphere is very claustrophobic. Before it was just the 'bar' of the Sherry Netherlands Hotel.) Our waiter turned my attention to the dessert table right in front of me and said 'Sir, you have the best view in the restaurant.' I pointed at my guest (gallantly, I think!) but she said she thought it wasn't unflattering to her, merely very Italian. I thought it actually sounded very Jewish to be that food crazy. If the waiter had been an Englishman he'd probably have pointed out the bottles of alcohol as the best view.

After lunch take a left turn (by the way if there's a paparazzi photographer outside I hope they've taken your picture both going in and out). As you walk in this direction, you'll see more culture in the windows of La Vielle Russie, which specializes in Russian antiques. They still have some quite nice pieces of Fabergé for sale, though fewer and fewer really good pieces seem to come on the market. The other great shop for Fabergé is Wartski in Grafton Street, London, otherwise you're most likely to find those unique fantasies from a bygone age only at an auction.

You'll pass probably the greatest toy store in the world for children and then some of the greatest toy stores in the world for adults, including Tiffany's. This occupies a whole corner and offers tableware as well as jewellery and silver for sale. Now go into Trump Tower, a shopping complex more like a marble palace, with a waterfall and five floors on top and Asprey's at street level (this Asprey's a little Americanized with a five-foot-high bejewelled gold bird as you enter) and what's probably the world's finest stationery from a branch of the Italian Pineider.

Don't linger in Trumps too long. Across the street Doubleday, the bookstore, have all the latest titles. Henri Bendel is a pretty little store just a few hundred yards down and for menswear especially look into Chari-Vari a few doors away. It has the latest in clothes, some of the brightest menswear in New York City – and some of the most expensive, sunglasses at $145.00! Although for expensive menswear in New York it's hard to beat Bijan (also in L.A. on Rodeo Drive), where you'll find a grey suede trenchcoat has been thoughtfully lined in grey mink! A set of crocodile luggage to put your purchases in will cost you $75,000. This shop doesn't like casual callers, you are expected to make an appointment to shop there. Reputedly, Frank Sinatra, Cary

Grant, Stevie Wonder, President Reagan and four kings all do.

You deserve tea by now, so head off past the Harry Winston store, cross the road past Bergdorf's to the Plaza. (All New York reminds me of songs: from 'Diamonds are a girl's best friend' comes 'Tiffany, Cartier, Harry Winston, tell me all about it'.) The Plaza is famed for tea among the potted palms and art deco elegance. After a delicious tea you should be feeling refreshed and ready for more: this is New York where nothing ever seems to shut down and neither must you so: how about the Museum of Modern Art now, or the Metropolitan, before going back to your hotel to change?

Your room will probably have a jacuzzi – I hate them, but if you want to try it check you know how to use it before getting in. Once you're in, it's too late to call for room service! That should set you up for the night. During the day you'll have heard if there's a really good show to see – a New York musical will have dancing like no other city, or watch out for the shows with the legendary stars.

If you've the time and the energy, have a drink at the Windows on the World Restaurant before or after the show – the view from the top of the World Trade Center is breath-taking, so too is the elevator because it goes so high and so fast and you need a drink at the top to get you back down. Then make your way to the hottest restaurant, which changes in New York almost week by week, almost certainly every couple of months. At the moment New York food is either Californian/Italian style with pizzas and pasta, or ethnic. L'Odeon, with the former dinner menu, has lasted longer than most and is still one of the rock business hang-outs – Paul Simon was there last time I was. Lola's menu is mainly Caribbean-inspired (there's a pianist); Sugar Reef and Indochine, all ethnic as you'd imagine, has the same palm tree wallpaper they have at the Beverly Hills Hotel. But tonight let's go to the hottest, Baton's. It's very California; a large bar filled with fun-seekers, carefully dressed down for the occasion. The food is slivers of raw tuna in sauce on skewers that makes you feel you're eating healthily.

Perhaps my favourite New York restaurant has to be the Four Seasons. It brings back every New York movie you've ever seen, even the ones it's not in, but New Yorkers wouldn't keep going there if it didn't maintain excellent standards. It's a treat just to experience the Picasso as you go in – it's enormous! Try for a poolside table – that's the chicest place to be. And yes, seriously, there is a pool in the centre of the restaurant. Don't try to catch your own fish, please!

And it's on to a club, where New York excels. A bit like London, you really need to know not only the hottest club of the moment but also which nights are the best where. Luckily you can get into many of the clubs free; charging you is a sign they don't much want you. Some of the smaller ones will ask if you're on the list – of course you are!

At the moment Palladium is what everyone's talking about. It's a huge ex-theatre space devoted to disco and owned by Steve Rubell whose Studio 54 was the first of its kind. I find, once I'm out on the town, one disco is seldom enough – in New York there's plenty to choose from. There's the Saint where you dance under a planetarium roof – and they have 'happenings' and Area have 'happenings' too, and exhibits. Of the smaller clubs there's Pyramid and the Milk Bar. Stringfellows is just like London, lots of chrome and lights, a mixture between Stringfellows club and the Hippodrome, very different from other New York clubs. And to finish off the evening what could be more New York/American than bagels and lox (that's cream cheese and smoked salmon on a kind of roll called bagel) at a café that's open all day.

Well, they admit they might close after five in the morning, but only if there are no customers about. Appropriately, it's called Lox Around the Clock and it is around the corner from the disco that's set in an old church and called Limelight. It dips in and out of fashion – you might like to try that too. I was going to say good night to you all! but, as the song goes, 'When a Broadway baby says "Goodnight", It's early in the morning.'

Sweet
Dreams

Paris

I once stayed at the Nova Park Hotel in Paris, which the *Guinness Book of Records* says was the most expensive hotel in the world. For around £500 a night my duplex suite had a drawing room with 'gold-plated' guest loo and a spiral staircase to the bedroom. Luckily, the seven-bedroom suite with its own private swimming pool was already booked. In the lobby they were selling Salvador Dali perfume at £5,000 a bottle. Returning from an exhausting shopping spree to this monster, which boasted shocking pink sun blinds all over, I was laden with parcels as I started climbing the huge chrome and glass staircase, better suited to a Busby Berkeley film. Suddenly even I couldn't believe my eyes. I would have pinched myself if I'd had a hand free, but there, coming towards me, and immaculate in tuxedo and black bow tie... was Charles Aznavour. And, yes, he is shorter than you'd expect. Give me the Ritz any day.

However, Paris needn't be expensive once you've got yourself there. Go for twenty-four hours and you'll get great value. If you can't afford the Ritz, the Crillon, the Georges V or L'Hôtel, there are masses of excellent cheap hotels – each of course offering a different experience.

Once you're there, make a plan. The Mona Lisa in the Louvre strikes me as the most disappointing painting ever, and it's small (talk about Charles Aznavour!) But you've got to see it once in your lifetime. (The best you can say about the Venus de Milo is she's 'armless.) For me, the greatest fun in Paris is the shopping. If it's Sunday, it's got to be the flea market. If it's a weekday, the shops are open – but you don't need money to go on a window-shopping spree. In Paris, the luxury status symbol car is the Rolls Royce; you can hire one, but they're hard to get hold of and with the crazy driving in Paris you're better off (just) walking. Ignore the kerb-crawlers; they'll probably go away – at least they don't pinch, as they do in Rome.

There are five main areas to see fashion, and you can see it all in one day if you've the stamina. En route, you may treat yourself to a 'bonne bouche' – the most delicious come from Fouquet and cost three or four francs. But have only one of these chocolates with enough calories to last you for miles!

First make for the Brasserie Lipp, your starting-off point for the Rive Gauche area. Don't be sidetracked into having a quick something there; it's hard to tear yourself away from its Olde Worlde charm, and there's the temptation of the Drugstore next door, and the Deux Magots opposite, and all the memories of Cocteau, Sarte and the literati legends the area holds. Not only are coffees expensive in Paris, they're also a ritual. If you stop now, you'll not get beyond Ted Lapidus on the corner, and beyond that there's Gianni Versace, Marcel Lassance (he reputedly dresses President Mitterrand), Alaia on rue de Bellechasse, Issey Miyake, Claude Montana, a huge Yves Saint Laurent and many more innovative designers beyond.

Now you've the taste of the latest looks, head for the Place des Victoires, an upmarket square with a charm all its own, statuary in the middle and some of the chicest shops like Thierry Mugler and Kenzo, Comme les Garçons, Yohji Yamamoto, Jean-Paul Gaultier, des Marithé and François Girbaud, whose label is 'Closed'. (My favourite jeans are 501s and Closed.) The best shop for gifts for the home, Au Bain Marie, is on one corner.

Then move on to Les Halles, where it's more street fashion – the boutiques come and go, in and out – but you must go up and down at least once on the extraordinary moving staircase that straddles the Pompidou Centre. Love it or hate it, you're given a unique view of Paris and its daily life, and the building is certainly spectacular. Hereabouts are all the fun shops, the second-hand clothes stores, the wilder and more affordable things, and though the shops open and shut the international stars (especially the Japanese like Kansai, the rock stars' favourite of the moment) stay on.

The next area is along the Faubourg St Honoré. You only need to come off this thoroughfare around the Place Vendôme and the Rue de la Paix where the jewellers vie to attract your attention. Van Cleef and Arpels, Cartier, Chaumet, Buccellati – and the Ritz Hotel in one corner. The service in these shops is sensational, and in the clothes shops too. I was once staying at the Ritz, and lost a button off my Ermenegildo Zegna blazer. The shop where I'd bought it is in the Rue de la Paix, so I asked there for a button. They insisted on putting it on, and wanted no payment. The Cartier here is almost too big; I prefer that in Cannes. (You come off the Croisette, all hot, and are instantly offered a drink, served on a silver platter, which makes parting with your money so much pleasanter. The glasses have Cartier initials in gold, and when I first saw these I determined that when I opened my shop clients would be offered if not champagne, coffee, from cups bearing my gilt initials. Our coffee is ever perked and ready!)

Back along the Faubourg St Honoré, the fashion names leap before you: Lanvin, Hermès, Sonia Rykiel, Pierre Cardin, Torrente, Courrèges, Loris Azzaro, with the Elysée Palace in the middle. If there's a crowd outside, it means the President is coming or going – very *Day of the Jackal*. I'm a great fan of Pierre Cardin, who comes up with brilliantly innovative ideas, and by grasping all the opportunities in his way has become one of the richest men in France – with all the power to distribute his designs that confers. It's said he now dresses Mrs Andropov. Some people argue his influence has weakened in some areas, but I'd suggest you check out his couture men's shop and the furniture shop, full of intriguing ideas. The Espace Pierre Cardin makes theatre-going more of an experience than just watching a performance.

The last area for fashion is around the Plaza Athenée Hotel, in the Avenue Montaigne, with several of the richest shops in Paris: Christian Dior, Valentino, Ungaro, Nina Ricci, Harry Winston, Hanae Mori, Jean-Louis Scherrer, Porthault for bed linen, where a pair of sheets and pillowcases could be £2,000 (embroidered, as much as £5,000!). You deserve that 'bonne bouche' now, and there's a Fouquet just opposite Dior. You can visit Pierre Cardin's couture house in a glorious classical French building, or you may want to go in search of the Swiss Village on Avenue de Suffren. This is a collection of antique shops – perhaps not the best place for bargains, but offering variety and lots in the French style.

No day in Paris is complete without a view of the Eiffel tower, and from there you'll see it, looming large. In one of the most romantic apartments I've ever stayed in, I woke up to see it perfectly framed in the bedroom window.

To see some painters, the Closerie des Lilas in Montparnasse is a charming place unique to Paris, ideal for a drink or a light supper. You may notice we haven't stopped for lunch. I seldom do. I might have a quick snack in Angélina, rue de Rivoli, because it's one of the last tea rooms left with romantic murals and lots of dowagers in perky hats. If I've time for a smart longer lunch, there's the Relais Plaza, no ordinary relais, being in the Plaza Athenée. Beauvilliers in Montparnasse would be wonderful for the fresh flowers even if the food weren't so remarkable. But there's no time for that and all the window-shopping. If you've still got the energy, wander around the Champs Elysées, or stop for a drink somewhere like the Renault Pub. (I can't say you haven't lived if you haven't had a drink in a car showroom, but try it just once.)

I love buying records in the Champs Elysées. A lot of people think French music is second rate, but I love Dalida and Charles Trenet. And back home on a dull day in London, light French music evokes the feeling of Paris as nothing else can. (Almost any star would love to play the Olympia in Paris, but few have done it as Dalida did. A fervent admirer booked the whole theatre, and had her do her whole show just for him!)

Paris nightlife means dinner first. If money's no object, go to Lucas Carton. Fashionable Paris diners are as fickle with their restaurants as with their designers. The really fashion-conscious are rushing off to Neuilly to the Café La Jatte, or to the brasserie Boeuf sur le Toit, recently completely revamped since its Cocteau heyday. But La Coupole seems to continue being trendy, and reasonably affordable. If you haven't been there, you must try it. In any other city a clientele composed of a mix of rich kids, glitz, fashion, business people, rock 'n roll – and tourists – would mean the food isn't serious. The meals are light by French standards, but no French meal isn't serious! And if the service is maddening, pretend that's part of the ambience.

The evening's just begun. At least one boîte, a disco, is a must. Régine's and Castel are for the chic, Les Bains, the Palace, Tango, Le Garage are places to let your hair down. I was in Le Garage one night and a neon sign lit up as I arrived, announcing 'Le Garage souhaite une bonne soirée à Ringo Starr'. How tacky, I thought – until seconds later, he swept by me.

For a romantic stroll, cross the Seine by its elegant floodlit bridges, and pause to admire the other illuminated buildings, especially Notre Dame. And for a late-night bite, there's a pizza store in the Champs Elysées that never seems to close. I usually end up having one on the way home after a great night. At three o'clock in the morning, they're the best in the world. And if the pizza gives you another burst of energy, there's always Keur Samba, which is a great boîte for four a.m.

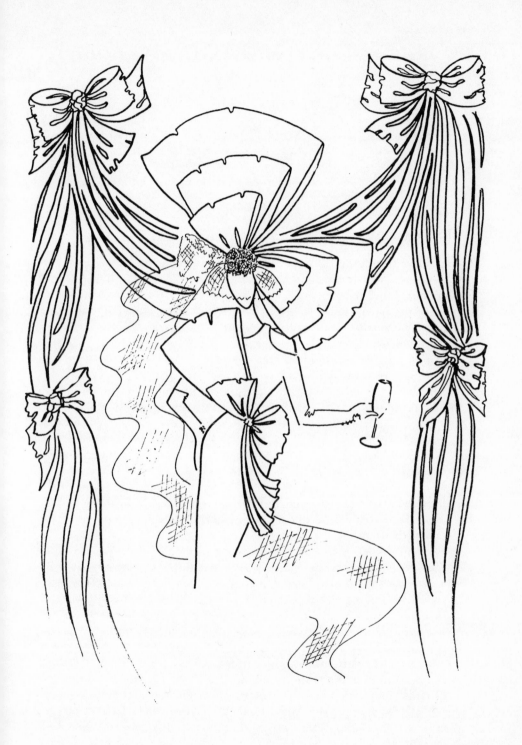

It's reputed to stay open till ten o'clock in the morning. Poor people of Paris, my foot!

Monte Carlo

Twenty-four hours in Monte Carlo would be a lovely treat, a long weekend even better, but don't be misled by the day trips to the capital. I find it extraordinary that many tourists can visit such a tiny Principality without actually scratching the surface of what makes the place, originally built for the rich and famous who still crowd down there each summer. Because of its fame, tourists flock into the wonderful old Casino in the town square with its dramatic architecture and symmetrically set out gardens. The really rich, meanwhile, gamble with their fortunes at the tables in the 'Summer Casino' down on the beach into the early hours. The old Casino is where you'll be directed by Monaco's immaculate private police force or whoever else you ask; if you have to ask the way, you're not in the Summer Casino league. The smart one is the modern one built on the beach. Men must wear smart suits to be sure of entry to the Summer Casino. Apart from that, all you need is your passport to get in. Girls have to be 'suitably' dressed, but the younger and prettier, the less they wear the better. If you don't want to gamble, it doesn't cost much to take a drink in the Casino.

The clue to Monte Carlo *de luxe* is this, that the best time to visit is in summer – the first two weeks in August are perfect. Some of the best spots only open for the summer, or change their winter venues as the day time tourists start arriving. The season reaches its climax in the week that ends with the Red Cross Gala, on a Friday night where the cabaret is likely to be provided by Frank Sinatra if he's in town. Although there are stunning apartment blocks, and newer hotels such as Loews (and that's pronounced like *l'oeufs*) vie with more traditional establishments such as L'Hermitage, in Monte Carlo there is just one hotel to be seen in, the famed Hotel de Paris. It has a Cartier on the corner and beneath it the most fabulous shops are arranged, Van Cleef and Arpels, Dior, YSL, Gérard, Hermès. You should take a light breakfast in a suite here before setting out to the Monte Carlo Beach Club. Although the hotel has its own swimming pool, shaded by a shell-shaped roof, it is to the Beach Club that 'everyone' heads, to be there by midday. The hotel runs a non-stop service to and fro throughout the day, in four London taxis: three black and one red. The Monte Carlo Beach Club is ill-named – the beach is actually not in Monte Carlo but just outside the limits in Cap Martin. The rich book cabanas here, equipped with bells for service – there's a jetty for friends to drop by in their motorboats for lunch, or you can set off for St Tropez. An invitation to the Byblos hotel there is always nice. The penthouse apartment has its own swimming pool. But even closer is Beaulieu, a perfect little trip along the stunning Mediterranean coastline could take you to the African Queen for some of the most exciting cocktails in the world and super pizza. But if it's your first time, you should lunch at the Beach; there are several restaurants to choose from, The Point being the most exclusive. Here a healthy little meander from the pool amongst the trees and flora cultivated above the rocks brings you to a commanding position at the furthest end of the Beach, perched above the sea.

My favourite lunch is simple, with the Mediterranean sweeping out before you, the delight of Monte Carlo rising above, beauty all around, the perfect meal where all you need to wear is a perfect suntan, is spaghetti, tuna and herbs, with a little wine mixed with Perrier. It's not quite the same but I often make the spaghetti at home – even without fresh basil it's a treat – and it's quick and *easy*.

Boil water with a spot of oil in it and put spaghetti in until it's al dente, which will give you time to open a can of tuna and get your plates etc. ready. Mix the spaghetti with a little oil or butter, pepper to taste and dried basil leaves (or mixed herbs if you haven't any basil) then stir in the tuna. I add a spot of Tabasco too, but I like things a little hotter!

Occasionally the splash of a diver or two reminds you why everyone is wearing swimsuits, though you're as likely to see women lunching here as fashionably as in any restaurant, with the most glamorous sunhats in the world, and the jewellery, while nothing in comparison to what's worn at night, is nevertheless not costume jewellery – but 24-carat swim costume! Men wear gold chains that might make you fear for their safety – chains thick enough to carry anchors on a fair-sized yacht! Your lunch will be delicious with enormous choices of salads, a speciality.

Life here is unpredictable. I was looking forward to a trip to the Eden Rock one lunchtime – a small party of us were all ready to go – but it had to be put off because the wife of the boat owner decided she had to be at the beauty salon by two o'clock because of that night's gala.

In the afternoon, treat yourself to a walk around the Olympic-size swimming pool – and join a game of backgammon in a friend's cabana before returning to the hotel to prepare for the real fun to begin! Several companies, especially jewellers, give amazingly lavish parties for guests in Monte Carlo, every evening during the height of the season. The exhibitions of gems are the most amazing in the world, the gems in cases only being rivalled by the gems worn by the guests at the private views. Monte Carlo is the only holiday resort I know where you really need your personal secretary to deal with the invitations! I remember one jeweller holding parties at the Hotel de Paris each night for a week, and each night he filled the showcases with even more fabulous sets of jewellery created around a different coloured stone, rubies, sapphires, emeralds and finally culminating in entirely diamond suites.

Because of the respect in which the Monte Carlo security is held, women walk unselfconsciously around the fashionable areas wearing millions of pounds of jewellery. There might be a party for an exhibit or an auction's private viewing. It was in Monte Carlo that I attended a Sotheby's auction where a record price for a single item of furniture (since broken) was achieved when on 25 June 1979, a Louis XV encoignière (corner cabinet) was sold for 7,600,000 French francs, then worth £835,165.

If you want a classic treat in a restaurant in August, go to the Hotel de Paris for dinner. The shimmer of crystal glints on the table, in the light of the huge ornamental chandeliers, and the beads of the couture dresses vying for attention is outdone by the mind shattering jewels – and in this miniature world of total inequity the odd man, including an Indian princeling or two, might catch your eyes with emeralds and rubies to dazzle. When it is not uncommon for a woman to wear £1 million of jewels, it makes you wonder what they did to deserve such stones. My goodness! Or, as Mae West said, 'Goodness had nothing to do with it.'

Afterwards, watch the rich and famous gather in the lobby of the Hotel de Paris or in the bar, making arrangements for the evening. Before they leave, those on their way to the casino rub their hand over the bronze horse in the lobby for good luck.

If you are invited to a dinner it could well be at the Pirate, a wild and fabulous restaurant along the coast towards Menton where the proprietor decides at the end of the meal what he'll charge for it, so a host never can tell! But if you want something a little quieter there's a restaurant up on the hill in the tiny village of Monaco, where you eat at tables on the tiny cobblestone streets lit by old street lamps and the natural light of the night. Before the meal you can wander around the

mediaeval parts of the village, look at the beautiful floodlit palace with its colourful guards on duty, and enjoy the view of the throbbing twinkling town and glittering port below.

Pinocchio's is a simple restaurant, which appears unpretentious. Laura Aitken, on my recommendation, took a friend there, only to find him very disgruntled at being in what he considered a rather rustic place – until he spied a fellow diner. It looks terribly like the Duke of Bedford, he kept saying; when he finally realized it actually was the Duke of Bedford he settled down to enjoy his meal.

In Monte Carlo a lot of things are done in the open air at night. Princess Grace inaugurated the now-famous concerts which are annually held in the beautiful courtyard of the palace. The orchestras are framed between the sweeping balustrades of the double staircase and even if you don't love classical music the romantic atmosphere of this setting – the painted murals and stucco and fairytale architecture, should convert you. Amazingly it's not necessary to book six months ahead for these concerts!

In the summer months in Monte Carlo they set up an open-air screen beside the casino, making it the most romantic cinema I know.

But perhaps you'd rather boogie? There's nowhere better than Jimmy'z, in the New Casino complex. Descend in a typically 'Régine's' style mirrored lift, to what I still feel is the most beautiful disco in the world. The view of the Mediterranean is enhanced here and there by fountains playing in the sea. There is an exhilarating mixture of the rich and famous and the beautiful, the young and old. It was here I saw Sophia Loren make a sensational entrance: everyone else vied with evening dresses of more exotic colours and yet more fabulous jewels; she wore plain black with a silk flower on a band around her neck. The evening before Gina Lollobrigida had shimmered away in a tight glittering gown, doing it quite differently!

One summer, when I was a teenager, I'd gone on to the original of Jimmy'z, Maona, after a birthday party in which the Beach Club Olympic pool had been drained especially to provide the disco floor! I ostentatiously danced with my 'lady' friend with my socks stuffed into the belt of my trousers. The new Jimmy'z only opened in the late 1970s, and we're both much more sophisticated now.

After you've gyrated on the dance floor, how about gambling in the Casino above? Don't expect to impress anyone with a flutter of a few hundred francs. Here the limits are high, tens of thousands of pounds change hands on the flick of a roulette ball, the turn of a card. Although the most extraordinary run at roulette I've ever seen, or am ever likely to, occurred on my first visit to a casino at Deauville. (My parents bought me a dinner suit when I was thirteen, they always wanted me to do grown-up things. I was taken to the theatre from a very early age because my mother thought it good for me, and better value to buy the extra ticket than have to pay for a sitter.) I was under age for entering a casino, not being twenty-one, but my parents were well known there. My mother lit a cigarette, put it to my lips and marched me inside. Here I was thrilled to find every expectation fulfilled – glitz and glamour. And there was even 007, Sean Connery. Suddenly I spied Brigitte Bardot relaxing with a friend, while her husband Gunther Sachs played roulette. There was quite a lot of excitement when his number came up, especially as he had the maximum bet on it. When he left the maximum bet on the same number, even this sophisticàted room held its breath. The atmosphere was electric when he won a second time, and left his bet on for the third spin of the wheel. (We're talking about winnings of tens of thousands of pounds each time; people took their chances by following his bet.) More chips had to be called for by the bank to pay his winnings and even Brigitte Bardot seemed to be drinking nervously. The ball came to rest; this time he'd lost. He instantly replaced the maximum chips on the same number. The crowd swelled around him, play ground to a halt elsewhere, Sean Connery looked on with an unBond-like admiration. When the croupier called 'No more bets,' an extraordinary hush fell on the room, the wheel spun, the ball rolled round, slowed and finally came to a halt. There was uproar – he'd got his hat trick! It was ages till enough chips were found to satisfy the winners. That was probably the closest I'll ever come to seeing the bank broken. When calm was finally restored, I put a small bet on my birthday number. It came up! I took off my winnings, which were only the equivalent of a few pounds, but seemed enormous to me, and since then I've never bet at roulette.

After you leave the Casino there's 'No Rock', the other Monte Carlo in spot, recently opened by Marianna Bjorg. If that doesn't get you, there's always some tiny café open for an early breakfast. Since you're only in Monte Carlo for 24 hours, you don't need to hire a car, but any longer and you should so that you can explore some of the other nearby delights of the South of France like the legendary restaurant, Le Moulin de Mougins, Roger Vergé's restaurant near Cannes, the birthplace of new French cooking, the Maeght foundations at St Paul de Vence, an incredible Centre for Modern Art, the extraordinary nightlife of Cannes, the more picturesque port of Antibes and there's the Hotel du Cap's Colombe d'Or. If you've got that car, now's the time as day begins to break to use it to explore the coastline and enjoy the breath-taking scenery. As the sun rises, the roads will start to fill and remain jam-packed till the end of yet another day.

Approaching Paddington '83.

London

It would be so lovely to have the sort of day out in London a tourist would. I'd want to start at Regent's Park, saying 'good morning' to the elephants at London Zoo, then walk across the park past several Nash Terraces and on to Baker Street. Hiding behind one of the unattractive commercial shop fronts is the fictitious home of Dr Watson and Sherlock Holmes. Halfway perhaps you should veer off to Dorset Street, into Chiltern Street (after a quick glance in the window of DS's hat shop perhaps?!) Then on to spend a few minutes in the beautiful but never overcrowded Wallace Collection in Manchester Square – sometimes it's so empty you feel quite at home with the Rembrandt self-portrait, the Cannallettos, even Turner watercolours, and, perhaps their most famous picture, the Laughing Cavalier. This must be one of the best-known paintings in the world, but if you ask people how many feathers are in that hat few can give the correct answer. In fact, it's none. The feathers one would expect to flourish on the brim of a Cavalier's hat are just not there; it is the sweep of the crown, and his extraordinary moustache which gives the picture its panache. If you don't believe me go see for yourself. There is a superb collection of armour, and another of French furniture, but don't linger because only a few hundred yards further on is Selfridges. Admire the art deco clock above the central main entrance and then take to South Molton Street where the boutiques show a selection of mostly the best of European fashions with some English too! Take a left turn, Claridges is on your right where Royalty entertain, and now head for the auction house Sotheby's in Bond Street. This usually affords some exciting viewing, amidst shops showing international essentials for the jet-set. The two fine furniture shops, Mallet and Partridge, have exquisite pieces with prices to match. I particularly liked a piece Partridge recently had in their window: a gilt Empire chair, upholstered in leopard-printed velvet, with arms in the form of female figures. Now comes a bevy of jewellers from Van Cleef and Arpels to Boucheron. In their midst at Asprey's, like at Tiffany's, you can buy playing cards or fountain pens, picnic hampers or a tiara. To your left runs Savile Row, still the Number One street in the world for men to buy a suit - and Cork Street, the centre of the modern art market in Britain. At the end of Bond Street, parallel to Burlington Arcade, art again mixes with fashion, and as you turn into Piccadilly you choose either the Royal Academy for culture - or Fortnum & Mason, renowned for its groceries. Or maybe you choose neither!

It's probably time for a drink and where better than the Ritz Hotel? It depends where you visit most - to some people the Ritz is in London, to some 'the' Ritz is in Paris. (The Paris Ritz is older and now a great deal of money is being lavished on it. Because the owners there feel the Ritz must have a swimming pool, for instance, they are building one, even if that does mean excavating below the foundations!) One thing is sure, the Palm Court in the London Ritz is unique.

Refreshed, it's now time to move on. Take a taxi or a red double-decker bus from outside the Ritz for a short ride to Knightsbridge - there's Harvey Nichols on the corner of Sloane Street. On a clear day you can almost see the famous square at the other end! And further along Knightsbridge you can't miss Harrods. Both these stores have fabulous window displays - the English excel at this. Many other countries could learn a lot from us here! You probably have just enough time to get to San Lorenzo in Beauchamp Place for a late lunch. Or, if you have time to nip into Harrods, remember to visit the Bread Hall if nowhere else - not only is it wonderful bread to buy, the aroma is mouth-watering. From San Lorenzo it's only a short walk to the Victoria and Albert Museum, the costume court is fascinating if you're interested in seeing costume throughout history, and the twentieth century is especially well documented too. Or you could take a short taxi ride to the King's Road to see what's happening in British fashion this very minute. Although punk certainly isn't the whole story, if you haven't yet seen a guy with twelve-inch spikes of orange or turquoise hair, here's where you will; and if you have the stamina for more fun British fashion, make a ten-minute dash by taxi to Kensington Market. More punk but much, much more besides; innovation and inexpensive.

Opposite Kensington Market, Hyper Hyper has more 'upmarket' stalls selling individual designer clothes, at more 'upmarket' prices! These shops shut around six o'clock, so make your way to the fairly recently-opened Covent Garden area, where you can enjoy a drink before the theatre. If you're taking a taxi ask your driver to point out the Albert Hall, although it's hard to miss, and Hyde Park Corner, and you can take a slight detour to Buckingham Palace, then up St James's so you go back into Piccadilly and get a view of Eros at Piccadilly Circus. And go via Trafalgar Square so you don't miss Nelson's Column, and the Landseer Lions! Covent Garden is convenient for most London theatres.

It would be a shame not to go to the theatre when in London. It offers arguably the best theatre in the world at the moment, and you're getting great value when you compare our prices to those in New York. But don't just think of the latest musical shows or comedies with well known television stars in. The National Theatre and other more serious offerings are worth your attention.

For a late meal go to Joe Allen's, where you can start star-spotting. Be warned, it's no good getting there too early because the actors and actresses who frequent it have to have time to take their make-up off. And here there is definitely a 'star-system'. The left-hand 'room' is the smart one, and 'stars' do not wait for their tables and they don't hang around the bar. Mere mortals may find they have to. If you want to keep up your image, don't! If you want to dance, ask the staff of Joe Allen's if they can advise where, because at present the real fun London club scene has got so crazy that each club only operates at full force one night a week. The clubs change venue with terrifying regularity, setting up house in a nightclub for several weeks, and then moving on. I went to a club, organized by the surreptitious handing out of printed cards by a committee among 'friends', and launched on a Thursday night in a Shaftesbury Avenue nightclub! I left well before the end of the evening but thought it had great potential. Turning up the next week I asked the bouncers at the door if the — Club was operating there. 'Not tonight and never again.' The big monster stared menacingly. I don't know what had happened but it must have been some party!

It's not true that everything shuts down by twelve o'clock in London. For a late-night snack, try the Bagel Factory in Brick Lane and wind your way back to the centre again via the river. You could even take further refreshment at the coffee stall on Chelsea Bridge. Here you'll get a mug of *real* English tea.

Weekending

If someone asks you to join a houseparty for the weekend, your first thought should be no! If not, then ask yourself *why*? Why do I want to spend the weekend with these people? Who'll be there? What will they expect of me? Will it be a pleasure or a pressure? (If these things aren't occurring to you, then you're either terribly thick-skinned – or a successful jet-setter, with a thick skin.)

Even if you're a couple (married or not), which gives you a bit of security and moral support, you should know your hosts quite well before you decide to spend a weekend with them. It's true that you never really know your friends till you've lived with them! There are, of course, happy exceptions! I've had hosts and hostesses who have unselfishly arranged amusing times for me, or left me alone enough to prove they honestly hoped I'd do my own thing. And I've stayed in homes so well staffed and so large that as long as I appeared for lunch and dinner no one took much notice of what occurred between.

But you've said yes. The house looked charming in the photos. Find out as much as possible before you go. Try to take a car with you, and not just for a get-away vehicle; you can take extra things with you as well as take a drive out occasionally. Make sure you've got a real escape route in an utterly foolproof excuse, which you deliver no later than your arrival (something like, 'My nephew's critically ill, and I'll have to phone the hospital occasionally' should do the trick).

I may sound cynical, but I've suffered. One of my first weekending disasters occurred when a rather pretentious (on reflection) girl asked me to spend the weekend with her at her parents' country place, which she described very grandly, while they were away in Spain. It turned out not to be the romantic seaside villa she had led me to imagine – it was in a very dull cul-de-sac where you could hear the neighbours pull back the curtains to get a better look! Not only was there no one to look after the house, it never had been looked after; and it was freezing cold with no obvious means of making it warm.

Worst of all, although she'd arrived early to get things ready, there was no food that could possibly see us through the weekend – no ingredients for perfect breakfasts or even one passable brunch. I lasted till the evening, then broke down. Surreptitiously I called another girlfriend, who agreed to come and rescue me the next morning. 'Bring some baked beans,' I said (yes honestly, it's true) and she did!

Later the Hampstead home of the seaside villa owners was (almost) burgled. They were watching television, and the burglars came in – but left without stealing anything. If that had happened before my weekend with their daughter, I'd have been warned.

78

Another disastrous time occurred when my hostess was having a clandestine affair with one of the guests. As I was a very good friend of her husband, I spent the entire weekend in a great moral quandary. It was pretty bad from the beginning, but the worst experience came when we drove to a beautiful lagoon one evening for a swim. I suddenly realized, as his swimming trunks floated by, that he was no longer actually inside them!

I've been to the South of France for the weekend and had my luggage lost on the plane. I've also been invited to the South of France to find when I got there that I was really there to advise on the decor – I wouldn't have minded so much if I hadn't been expected to traipse round the super-marché doing the shopping as well!

Other problems for me on weekends are that I'm not good early in the mornings – that's about 11.30 on Sundays; I'm not at all interested in sports: golf bores me and I can't hit a ball at tennis or squash though I love swimming (but generally I need the sun shining down on me) and I hate washing up in other people's homes. Still, I do occasionally try to set up houseparties.

My advice is first, choose whom you're inviting *very* carefully. Don't expect people to fall in love – you're more likely to witness the start of divorce proceedings, if my experience is anything to go by. Don't be worried if you think you're hearing footsteps in the corridor during the night; the host of a houseparty must learn to turn a blind eye to a lot of things. The more you don't notice, the greater success you'll have.

If you're able to offer most of the following you may be on to a winner – (a) sunshine (b) regular feeding (c) separate rooms for each person/couple (with double beds for all if possible) (d) plenty to drink (e) non-compulsory entertainment, books/videos/games/television/ radio (f) housework only if someone really wants to do it as therapy. If you've guests in your own home you should put a few flowers and clean towels to make the place welcoming, a fresh bar of soap, if possible a radio or personal stereo. Perhaps a selection of books and the telephone should be pointed out as being available, a packet of tissues by the bed.

The perfect guests will have brought the right clothing, their personal stereo and a book, and a gift. (It may be no more than a jar of jam or a box of chocolates, but it shows the host or hostess their efforts are appreciated.) Perfect guests will also offer to help, and be prepared to follow and lead as required. The host and guests should all try to adopt unselfish attitudes – but it's not that easy!

My friend Nancy Delman once rented a house on the beach on Long Island for a month. We arranged the first houseparty and went on ahead to get everything ready. Feeling Scott Fitzgeraldish, I had great expectations for a super weekend with an amusing set of stylish and charming guests. Imagine our horror when we saw the house – it was dreary, like something out of a Western ghost-town. I half expected the sheriff to be riding in on his horse-drawn buggy . . .

I left Nancy to unpack, and rushed round to get flowers. There weren't enough in the local shops so I bought all the balloons I could find and, cutting down on cooking time, we blew up masses of balloons and strung them all on to the porch. Then we started on the inside, dusting away cobwebs and arranging flowers and more balloons, draping a spare sheet over the settee to brighten the room. By the time the first guests had arrived the house was transformed, at least it looked welcoming, and a wonderful weekend was had by all. That's really the watchword for giving the successful weekend: make your guests feel terribly welcome, without feeling smothered.

To be a really generous/efficient host, how about leaving an electric kettle and some tea bags in the room, a bottle of mineral water and a small tin of biscuits – and some Alka-Seltzers (something no guest likes to have to ask for). If you've time and know your guests well enough, choose books and a magazine or two for them. Things to spoil yourself in the bath are always a delight. If a room isn't often used, make sure it is aired and smells nice.

Always provide plenty of hangers – remember men use hangers with a trouser bar – and supply these in the cupboard. A good quantity is better than one or two beautifully padded; provide plenty of spares for your guests' clothes. It's flattering to you if they've decided to bring a lot of changes of clothes! If there is anything in the house you don't want your guests to see, remove it, or lock it away.

If you want people to come and go on their own, give them keys to allow them to get in late at night. Put them on an extra large key ring so it's more difficult for your guests to leave with them at the end of the stay, and suggest they leave the keys on the hall table when they're not out.

I've stayed in houses where there is a printed form for your breakfast, and you leave this outside your door, just like at an hotel – but I'm told this is pretty rare. Many households expect you to appear downstairs for breakfast (you don't have to be formally dressed, but don't go down in your pyjamas unless you know your hosts would expect you to), but you may be invited to take your breakfast in your bedroom. Your host should confirm the arrangements the night before. If you are being brought breakfast in bed you should not move out of your room before breakfast is served to you; quite clearly, you might not be welcome downstairs!

If you're staying with friends and feel that either you or your host or hostess needs a discreet 'do-not-disturb' warning system which won't embarrass anyone, you can use the shoe code. At its simplest, a pair of shoes outside a door means do not enter. (Whose shoes, and how arranged, can say a great deal more.)

petit Moulton from
my window
Jany 1st 1986.
David Shilling.

Going out

I always say I hate going out, and June's the worst month of all in London. This year, June 1 was on a Sunday and there was a fabulous garden party for Judy Campbell's seventieth birthday, with her daughters Linda and Jane Birkin, Sir John Mills, etc... The next day, I had nine invitations but - because I hate going out - I accepted only five of them. They ranged from a party at Cartier in Bond Street and the opening of an exhibition of Royal photographs by Lord Lichfield to the opening of an exhibition of bronze sculptures in the peace and tranquillity of the Leighton House Museum by Holland Park, which seemed almost rural by comparison. (When Régine opened her doomed nightclub in that area, someone prophesied its failure: 'It'll never succeed...it's too far from Town!') The next night offered much of the same, except that it ended with a stag party that started in Dean Street and disintegrated, I gather, long after I left. By Wednesday, I'd still the stamina to go to a special viewing of the Cecil Beaton exhibition at the Barbican, organized by the designer David Bentheim. I was so engrossed in the photographs I forgot to leave for a dinner party, and ended up being thrown out by hefty Barbican officials, along with a dozen or so friends including Lord and Lady Settrington, so we made our way to Fortnum & Mason for champagne and Mont Blanc meringues with marrons glacés. Bang went another night's sleep. Sadly, I had to miss Katie Rabett's wedding in Canterbury Cathedral, but the week continued to its climax in a party given by Chris Cazenove and Angharad Rees, with guests serenaded by violinists, more salmon, more meringues and cream and lots of bubbly and beautiful people. A fitting end to the first week of June, and a good omen for the rest of the month with racing, polo, tennis, rowing and music parties still to come.

In the second week of June, the Grosvenor House Hotel in Park Lane had organized a David Shilling week, at which videos and live models showed my hats, as guests ate and drank from a menu I'd designed. It was great fun choosing all the food - and the drink! I wanted everything to be as tasty and delicious as it was attractive. Who said there's no such thing as designer food and drink? It's not surprising then that if you ask almost any celebrity at a party what their idea of a perfect evening is they'll say 'stopping at home'. They won't always mean with the wife, or husband, or alone. Some might even want just to watch television, others play with their stereo or pursue a hobby. And it might be that when companies are willing to pay several thousands of pounds for a celebrity to make a 'personal appearance' that it takes

the gilt off the gingerbread of going out, or perhaps puts too much gilt into it. One of the best things about being well-known is that you do get invited out a lot more. You don't have to be rich or famous, though that helps! (If you find you've become a catch, it's only fair to warn your host or hostess if you're not able to attend a party – otherwise he or she will be telling all the early arrivals how they'll enjoy meeting you, what fun you are... And you're probably lying in bed with the television on and one hand holding the telephone or a lover.)

Anyone can become a 'must' at a party – being single is an asset. Being decorative or amusing helps too. You aren't going to be invited out a lot if, when you get there, you sulk in the corner; this only worked for James Dean. He had a lot else going for him, and he only did his sulking when it was totally appropriate to do so – a talent in itself! You may just be planning to arrive late and make a grand entrance, but this has to be done with great charm. Lady Rothermere once arrived at my house at around eleven o'clock for a drinks party for a hundred people that should have ended at nine. She managed to revive the party for a further two hours – finally with no guests remaining, just me and the hired help. At least she arrived on the right evening!

If the doorbell rings around the time you've invited people for, but on the day before or after a party, beware: it's probably guests who've mixed up the dates. One couple of friends keep doing this to me (and to others) – once they turned up an entire week late. Their unexpected arrival sometimes creates wonderful spontaneous parties. Mostly they get away with it because they're not only beautiful but also rich and titled.

Theoretically, after a drinks party you can always get an early night if you want to, though usually you're asked to join people for dinner afterwards and I, like many others, find it very hard to say 'no' – especially at parties. I'll always retain the happy memory of a wonderful drinks party at the American Embassy in London. (The Ambassador, Walter Annenberg, was a very distant cousin of mine, but I was still his closest 'English' relative.) After the guests, who were all seriously successful and high-powered in their fields, had had their fill of the champagne and canapés, the Renoirs and the Van Goghs, the Bonnards and the Monet, and had departed, supper on trays was taken upstairs for the Ambassador and his wife – you see, everyone loves their TV dinners!

This doesn't mean it isn't great to go out. If you care about your appearance, though, you'll want to look your best. Someone who had not seen me for a couple of years, and maybe even five, once said to me, 'You really look great; just the same as ever, but I suppose nowadays it takes a little longer!'

People who live and work in the same town or city are tempted to go out straight from work. But for a really good night out, I recommend going home first. Run a warm bath, treat yourself to something that smells good, and splash plenty in. It needn't be the most expensive perfume in the world – you could even choose your own by combining essences that you like – and it certainly shouldn't be asses' milk. (I can't imagine it, can you?)

If you're feeling economical, buy a bag of cheap bath crystals in a colour which goes with your bathroom and put them in an attractive dish; or borrow your baby's 'Matey' – I'm told that can make a busy mother feel like Felicity Kendal. In fact, if you're in a frivolous mood, nothing beats the foam – as many bubbles as you feel like and some more in a glass of champagne for the extravagant.

My fondness for baths seems to be well known; recently I was phoned by a television programme (they'd heard I had a fabulous bathroom) and asked what I thought constituted the perfect bath. Only then did they ask me to be filmed in one! I had a good pair of swimming trunks and a recent suntan – so I thought, why not?

I seemed to remember hearing actors and actresses who'd been filmed in a bath complaining how cold the water got, and how after the third reshoot the skin became prune-like, so when the film crew began running the water I told them to make sure it was good and hot. When I finally got in, the water felt lovely and warm as I sunk under a foot of foam. Then they turned the lights on, and slowly the temperature seemed to rise – by the end I felt like a lobster must when boiled. My advice to anyone else being filmed in the bath is keep it cool!

One of the best things about a real bath is that it's one of the few places where one doesn't have to worry about what to wear.

It was a horrid feeling when I was first thrown in a jacuzzi. It was on Long Island Sound, at a fabulous house straight out of *The Great Gatsby*, with beautiful lawns sweeping down to the waterside, and a pier with white wrought-iron work. Next to the huge swimming-pool was a wooden tub into which I was not altogether voluntarily lowered. Overwhelmed by this novelty and the wealth of my hosts, I suddenly felt a joke was being played on me, and that this tub was in fact not for people but part of some giant new barbecue set, probably for cooking sausages when your hundred favourite friends come round for a Sunday brunch. I screamed to be hauled out, and I've never been impressed by jacuzzis ever since. I'm glad to hear now that it's becoming generally thought that they're actually breeding grounds for germs and most unhygienic.

I'm lucky because I get invited out to all sorts of parties, and they're all so different. Music people like noisy crowds, tight clothes, denim, black lace and leather. They search for 'unexpected' venues, or take over the 'smartest' clubs and gyrate till late. The trouble with music business parties is they're all so predictable, people shouting to be heard over the sound systems, everyone calling out something, clothes too tight, too much make-up and wild hairdos – but they're great, once in a while.

If you want to be a music tycoon I can help. First adjust your watch. The difference between music people and the rest of the world is that they get up later, and stay out longer. With actors you won't get home till two a.m., with musicians you might not get home at all! Don't call them in the morning, they'll be sleeping. Once you've made this adjustment there's not much else essential. If you like you can grow your hair, bleach and dye it, or have it almost shaved off. You needn't spend much money on your clothes, but they must be tight – and music people tend to be terribly skinny on the whole. What they eat may be fattening (fast foods, pizzas and Coke, McDonalds and Chinese), but they don't eat regularly. The real difference I've noticed between middle-of-the-road and heavy metal is the quality of the leather.

Only music superstars are into designer labels, Kansai clothes and haute cuisine – after all, you've got to be a Rock 'n Royal to afford to be!

Art gallery parties are quite something else. At the upmarket ones, centred around Cork Street, or the National collections, or Christie's or Sotheby's there will be more critics than artists, and even more paintings and cheque books. The size of the spread will be in proportion to the name of the artist – and the red dots that denote those paintings sold will be an indication, too.

At the 'struggling artist' end, the parties get much more laid-back. There's a literati-glitterati set that attends regularly to the cultural life between Fulham and Westbourne Grove, and occasionally they'll expound and explain and sometimes even look at the art. Less typical was the private view given by Sophie Parkin, Molly's daughter. (Molly is a dear friend, who has bought many of my more outrageous hats over the years. She once excitedly told me she was putting me in one of her novels. When the book came out, I read it avidly; by the time I reached page 140 I realized I wasn't to be the hero, but I thought my cameo role could still count for some of the novel's certain success. Which steamy sub-plot would I feature in, I wondered, hoping secretly that my performance would astonish friends and detractors alike. Then there I was, in black on white, in two lines – making the hat for the mother of the bride!) I made my way to the art gallery, below a hairdressing salon 'off' Carnaby Street, and furnished like a cross between an old-fashioned barber's shop, with huge leather chairs that

swivel up and down, and a post-nuclear holocaust – all the mirrors were broken, and the walls slopped with black paint.

Downstairs, the art gallery throng milled about with almost total disregard for the walls and I noticed something else for sale: an eighteen-inch-long bomb, with its metal tag a little smudged so that all I could make out was 'If this bomb is unexploded, put back the...' There were religious candlesticks, beautifully enamelled red fountain pens for £5.95, a huge round glass dining table with goldfish swimming within it – and Molly, the sex blockbuster writer, flamboyant in feathers and a purple and yellow beaded shawl. There were hangers-on and groupies, dancers, music people, designers, a whizz kid of the fashion scene in shaded velvet (redcurrant to clash with his hair)... I had a chat with Barbara Halanicki about Japan, left and went to a late-night session at a photographic studio.

Photographers' studios are like one long party: music blaring, lights, cameras, action! I had sent along hats, I'd pestered my florists for exotic blooms and leaves. I'd bought strawberries because we had so many black and white hats I thought a touch of colour might add something; there were several changes of clothes, for the model, all designed by me, from a black sequinned evening dress with a strapless top, slinky to the knees and ending in a whoosh of silver lamé, to an electric blue boob-tube and mini-skirt, fur stoles and several pairs of long gloves...

I staggered up the stairs with a few more props and obligatory bottle of champagne to find an anxious make-up artist, Filofax open, desperately phoning a model friend because the booked model hadn't turned up. The photographer, who was normally black, was ashen – and his assistant looked as nervous as anyone would who felt she might have to model if no one else turned up. She shrank to 4ft 11 when I waved a huge leaf from an exotic plant and asked if she had good shoulders. At least then she could hold the leaf in front of her face as a kind of fan. When the model eventually did turn up, with no make-up on, I'd have probably gone along with the assistant. Several hours make-up and lighting later we achieved a shot that's already been seen as far away as the *Los Angeles Herald*. But all that effort for just one head and shoulders shot. Think of that as you flick through a magazine at the hairdresser's or the dentist's.

For that old feeling of 'going out to the movies' why not get your video' sorted out? Hire or buy the film of your choice, and show a few shorts before: holiday films, cartoons, whatever you fancy. Set a time for the performance and then go out of the house. Lock the door behind you and grab a quick meal, even a McDonald's and a milkshake – 'Hurry up! The film starts at eight sharp.' Have your popcorn and your drinks ready, and away you go back to the house. (A canny wife could supplement her housekeeping money here!) Oh yes, and take the phone off the hook and determine not to answer the doorbell. The greatest advantage is at the end of the evening – no traffic jams before you get home!

A great *free* entertainment worth going out for in almost any capital city (apart from the obvious ones like window-shopping, car-spotting, and tracing the homes of the rich, famous and infamous, alive or dead) is star-spotting. This can be done by visiting restaurants, though that's expensive; or at nightclubs or openings, but you have to wait for nightfall. During the day you can still see stars! (In London, try hanging around the BBC, for a start.) In one day, I met Ian Ogilvy, who was stuck on his bike at traffic lights in Oxford Street; he was wearing a white jacket, but he was still unnoticed as we talked. A friend swears she was coming away from the stage door of *La Cage aux Folles* after the matinée and saw Cliff Richard and heard him say to his companion, 'When you see ours it's completely different – it's high-tech!' (*Time* the musical, presumably!) And later the same day she was in John Lewis and heard a man say 'I loved your show' to a somewhat surprised Lulu on the escalator. Then, on my way home, Chrissie Hinde (a fabulous singer) was just popping out of an antique shop.

If you want to see members of the Royal Family, apart from at the Highland Games, the Derby and Royal Ascot, the best places are premieres or charity performances. Arrive before the time the performance is due to take place; the earlier you are, the better view you'll get (and there'll probably be plenty to see while you wait as red carpets are rolled out and preparations made). Bad weather doesn't deter avid watchers of the Royal Family, so try and make sure you're warm and dry enough; and help your chances of a good view by finding out which way the Royal car will come.

Members of the Royal Family never give autographs; but other stars do, and most are quite happy to if approached the right way. It's insulting to ask anyone to sign a really dirty scrap of paper, but most celebrities will sign an autograph unless there's such a crowd that things might get out of hand. If you want a signed photograph, give the celebrity your name and address written on a piece of paper and ask for one. (If you have a photo give it to them in a stamped, self addressed envelope.) If you want to take a photograph, ask politely – most will stop briefly, particularly if it's at a function where professional photographers are present. After all, they're all done up and expecting it, aren't they? But don't expect anyone to wait while you put a new roll of film into your camera.

I once went to interview the Lord Mayor of London for my school newspaper; I was only twelve, and had a brand-new tape recorder. We did the interview – imagine my mortification when I tried to play it back, immediately afterwards, and found I'd got nothing on tape. I had the cheek to ask him if we could do it all again, and he actually agreed! But not everyone can be expected to be so accommodating. What happens if you spot a star and make an approach in Safeways is totally unpredictable.

On the other hand, you must respect people's privacy. I was being interviewed for the *Los Angeles Times* by Bevis Hillier in the bar of the Beverly Wilshire Hotel, when suddenly he pulled out his camera and snapped me. Within seconds, and as if from nowhere, a guest bounded over and grabbed the camera, saying, 'You shouldn't take photographs in here!' I didn't recognize him or his female companion so I don't know what his problem was, but I am sympathetic because I hate finding myself in a semi-private place with flashbulbs popping all around me, even if the results are only intended for the family album. One of the best things about going to the Chelsea Flower Show is that you can be sure the cameras aren't aimed at you; the photographers are much too absorbed by the plants.

For the bravest – gate-crash and have a good night out. A friend, who is now the head of a huge advertising agency, used to put on 'black tie' and enjoy the smartest functions in West End hotels. In theory, all you do is turn up at a hotel around 7.30 and look confident. After all, there are always guests unknown to their hosts at these occasions. ('Are you on the bride's side, or the groom's?' 'Yes!' is the correct answer.) Nearly always, someone doesn't turn up for dinner, so you take their place. A buffet supper is of course easier. Hints: never take a coat or umbrella, have matches to light people's cigarettes and cigars, offer to get drinks, and you'll be everyone's friend. Don't take cigarettes – over-friendly – and after all, what are you there for but to enjoy other people's hospitality? Finally, if something appears to be going wrong, retire to the lavatories, and if necessary stay there till it's safe to leave.

Theatre

Have you ever sat in a box in the theatre? Quite often when tickets for a show are hard to come by, a box is still available – although it may mean paying for four or six seats. But can't you and your friends use them? I'll admit the view is often not so good, especially if two of you have to sit in the back; but it does make you feel grand and certainly gets you noticed. Even if you're not rich and famous, you can always play it up a bit – wear dark glasses and rock star type clothes – or simply go dressed up. A man could wear black tie and a woman cocktail or evening dress. You could take your own bit of theatre to the theatre.

I've always liked taking a box because, as I said, it's sometimes the only way to get seats, and because if a party of us go it usually makes a great evening out, whether or not it's a great play. It feels a little as if you and your friends are watching the action just outside your drawing room window, from the comfort of your favourite chair. One night I went with friends to *On the Twentieth Century*, a musical about the famous train. I'd rushed to the theatre to get the tickets in the afternoon. 'No tickets,' they said. 'Have you a box?' I asked. Yes, they had, but did I mind if just a few minutes of the action took place from it. I nodded – my car was double parked – I didn't really think about the implications of what they'd said, paid for the tickets and got back to the car two seconds ahead of the traffic warden. They were probably joking anyway. I didn't give it another thought.

That evening we arrive at the theatre, take our seats, the performance begins – when suddenly the back door to the box opens and I'm the only one who has the slightest idea of what's going on. My dear friend Carole Steyn (an artist with works in Warsaw Museum, who usually gets the wrong end of the stick) asks Keith Michell to leave the box. Luckily he doesn't, as the spotlight shines on our box and he manages – just – to get out his lines, whilst pandemonium rages around him.

When I was a teenager I once managed to get a box to see Spike Milligan in his hugely popular show, I think it must have been during half-term. Just about the time the lights should have gone down there was a lot of hustle and bustle about in the corridor behind us as some latecomers arrived to take their seats; and then, suddenly, a whole row of the stalls below us started filling up – one by one the faces seemed familiar. The atmosphere in the theatre became electric as almost the entire Royal Family took their seats, accompanied by Peter Sellers. Imagine Spike Milligan seizing the opportunity to ask Peter Sellers, 'Why does the Duke of Edinburgh wear red/white/blue braces?' Peter Sellers, standing in the stalls, 'I don't know, why does the Duke of Edinburgh wear red/white/blue braces?' The answer was entirely lost in the roars of the audience.

Opening nights are always early. I recently went to one at the Duchess Theatre; there was a party afterwards, so Alice Rubicez, an opera singer, and I decided to walk across Covent Garden to it. But just as we reached the Opera House it started to drizzle. Well, I noticed that there were lots of people hanging around and quickly realized it was an interval. I suggested to her that we made our way inside to the bar to get out of the rain! We had a very nice drink before continuing the journey – I thought I'd discovered a rather good wheeze, until I found us 'exposed' in a gossip column later that week.

(Not that you should believe all you read – I once went to the opening of a Chinese restaurant, and was told to take the chopsticks home as a gift. Imagine my shock when I read on a diary page some days later that I was among those suspected of stealing the hundred pairs that had disappeared. I was in good company: other suspects included Julian Lloyd Webber, Angharad Rees, Gerald Harper, Baron Steven Bentinck and Angie Best.)

If you go to a first night because you've a friend in the cast, it's a lovely idea to send a little gift of flowers, or a card, backstage before the show starts. Don't go yourself! (If you must, do remember it's a tradition in the theatre to say 'break a leg', *never* to wish anyone good luck.) After the show, you should give them time to get a bit organized, then make your way to the stage door. You may be able to go in straight away, or you may be asked your name first. Always try to be sensitive: nobody wants to be told they were bad on any opening night. If you must be helpful, put it off till at least the next day. Dressing rooms are normally tiny – huge stars get bigger dressing rooms, but there's less space as they have more friends! And even more flowers! Don't overstay your welcome, and don't hang around waiting to be asked to the 'cast' party if you haven't already been. They aren't always that great anyway. The actors get nervous and turn up late. In productions where there are tensions amongst the cast these tend to magnify when it comes to the party. I once went to a lavish buffet dinner at Maxim's: it spread over several rooms, each one being hosted by one star – and you moved from one to another at your own peril!

When I go to the theatre, I like to have a bottle of champagne in the interval: if the play's good it makes the second half even better, if it's not it makes the second half more bearable. It's not worth struggling to the bar to get a drink in the interval. People in the know order their drinks for the interval on their arrival at the theatre, and collect them from the side – avoiding the crush entirely. I usually order an extra few glasses, because there always seem to be friends around who've not ordered drinks beforehand, and so an interval becomes a little party. This has only backfired on me once. I'd taken Tessa Dahl (the actress daughter of the writer) to the first night of Rowan Atkinson's one-man show. As I stuggled with opening the bottle during the interval, Tessa became deeply engrossed in conversation with Michael Parkinson. Suddenly there was the most almighty pop and champagne was flowing everywhere – but especially over what had been Michael Parkinson's light grey suit! I apologized profusely, I really don't know how it had happened. It is a fact, though, that I've never been asked on a Parkinson chat show since!

The etiquette of eating and drinking in the theatre is strange. I love popcorn in the cinema – why never in the theatre? Recently an older person told me she was going to the first performance of the cinema with a friend, and taking sandwiches; this reminded me of going to the cinema long ago with my grandmother and aunt, and having sandwiches. Apparently that was once quite commonplace. Now there are hardly any theatres left that serve tea on a tray at theatre matinées – and very few theatres offer coffee served in your seat during the evening interval. I know they still do at Eastbourne.

Still, it could be worse here. In New York you usually get your drinks served in plastic cups!

Restaurants

If you want a table at a fashionable restaurant you have to book. A pretentious friend (whom I no longer see) used to book tables in the name of an Italian Prince. Acquiring a bogus title seems easy. There is the story of a British socialite who wanted to make a great name for herself in America. Not content with being the Honourable Mrs, she just stuck Lady in front of her name and it was widely accepted. However, when her husband recently succeeded to a title, it meant they changed their surname too. The Americans were completely baffled by this and she lost all credibility as a result. My cousin Phillipa (who married Sir Henry Phillips and so became Lady Phillipa Phillips) always says that for her the greatest thing about getting married was how much better the service in her local greengrocer's became. As she enters they love to shout out, 'Good morning, *Lady* Phillips!'

Try saying, as you arrive at a restaurant, 'Nice to see you again' – even if it's your first time there. (If a doorman greets you with 'Nice to see you again,' *never* reply 'But I haven't been here before.') This is a useful phrase if you turn up somewhere fully booked without reservations.

A good restaurant is one that's cheap enough to make you want to go back again that week, and has enough warm and interesting faces to make you feel you're at a good party. At my favourite of the moment you can get a drink, a bowl of pasta and maybe some ice-cream after, for less than the price of a parking ticket. Leaving there one evening I spoke to Wayne Sleep – he'd just had all his hair cropped and bleached blond for his role in *Cabaret* ('I've determined to be as different as possible from the Joel Grey character'), Adrian George the painter, Una Stubbs and Mike Nolan – and that was just getting past the three tables nearest the door. Soon it will get too well known, more expensive, and we'll be on the lookout for a new venue.

I'm not sure if they just put all the most famous people at the front of the restaurant – or if it's even more fun at the back. I remember the first time I went to Mortons in Los Angeles there I had been warned by staff at the British Consulate how important it was to be seated in the right part of an LA restaurant – but I didn't know which part that was.

The girl I was with was looking wonderful – very shades of Krystal – Californian long blonde hair, and high-heeled patent shoes showing off long, long legs draped in black satin. She was acknowledged by the waiter, who said our table wouldn't be a moment. As he disappeared, I seized the chance to ask her which bit was the best. She murmured something about being in front of the potted palms . . . Suddenly, there was the maitre d', and we were being bid to our table, past the front tables full of smiling diners and then we reached the palms. To be honest, I wasn't sure what to do. I thought our table could well be too far towards the back of the restaurant, but I didn't see an empty alternative. As we stood by the table for a moment, I wondered what on earth I should do now. I've walked out of films, plays, I've walked out of restaurants for bad service, but what do you say if you're not happy with the position of your table? I looked round again – and saw Joan Collins and Jeffrey Lane, her publicist, at the very next table. I sank thankfully into my seat. The dilemma of what one might do if shown to the wrong side of the restaurant is as yet unsolved!

If restaurant service is bad, complain. If the service is rude, don't be rude back – refuse to pay your bill. To me, a restaurant isn't giving good value if all you've achieved is not having to do the cooking for one night!

There are very few restaurants round the world that offer sensational meals and service, and because of their high prices you're unlikely to see young and beautiful people there – more likely will be lots of tourists and middle-aged businessmen on expense accounts dining out with their wives, or perhaps with real secretaries. (Generally, a businessman doesn't take his young mistress to such a restaurant for fear of meeting other business colleagues – who probably would also rather have brought their mistresses along while discussing the latest wheeling and dealing. Being a mistress is, I gather, not educational.)

It's said that top Parisian restaurants have begun to impose an informal quota on the number of tourists they'll serve. If you have a problem booking a table in Paris, get someone with a French accent and a French-sounding name to book it for you.

Finally, beware of swopping gossip – wherever you are. A visiting American friend wanted to go to Mr Chow in Knightsbridge, a Chinese restaurant that does wonderful seaweed (the Los Angeles Mr Chow is, I think, even better), and we settled down to a wonderful juicy gossip – names, details, lots of background. Suddenly, as we reached the dessert, a woman from the next table swung round. 'Hi, Nancy,' she shrieked. My friend had been eavesdropped on by her next-door neighbour from New York!

Rich food

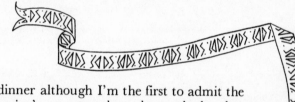

I love having people to dinner although I'm the first to admit the food's terrible and the wine's no more than cheap plonk - but there's always lots of it, and Perrier for those who don't drink alcohol. I can't cook cordon bleu, or rather haven't the time and the inclination. I was faced with a dilemma a couple of years ago when my friend Baron Philippe de Rothschild was coming for dinner. He made Mouton what it is today; at his table there are printed menus at luncheon and dinner, and he serves a different wine with each and every course. Each wine is a superb complement to the dish, an exquisite vintage, each bottle valued at several hundred pounds though many of the wines are - literally - priceless. He'll offer, to conclude, a choice of his private brandies or cassis, which because of some licensing laws cannot even be bought!

What wine do you serve? I decided to carry on as usual - cheap plonk was the only answer. If I served 'proper' wines, the food wouldn't be up to them.

I think food should be instant and quick, like the spaghetti I served that evening. I chop and fry together an onion, some tomatoes, mushrooms, raisins and honey, adjusting the quantities to make enough sauce to serve however many people I'm cooking for. If it looks on the dry side, I add tomato ketchup or puree... Philippe was delighted with it: it was such a change from the rich food he'd had for luncheon at the French Embassy. And he's been back for more since.

My rules for making dinner a treat are few but radical. I hate long formal tables. Round are always better. Six is an awkward number for conversation to flow, so if there are more than five of us I use two tables (I have a fold-away Regency rosewood table, but the humblest card table, covered with a pretty cloth, would do). If there are seven people, I put three on one table and four on the other. This seems to avoid those uneasy moments you get when eight people at the same table all stop talking together, and no one is brave enough to start the conversation again. I always split up people who've come together, unless it's very inappropriate (newly-engaged couples, agoraphobics - that sort of thing); and I definitely separate married couples. It's my experience that husbands and wives, even the very richest, always get to see enough of each other. Don't assume that a couple living together for several years would choose your dining table to learn more about each other - indeed, watch out if they have! I make sure everyone has a chance to meet by swopping a couple of guests over at pudding time; this prevents anyone having to put up with a bore all evening, and usually revitalizes the conversation. By the time coffee is served, both tables start to mingle.

I drink less coffee now, but I once thought one of the things I'd miss most on a desert island would be a coffee machine. I have one at home and one at work, and one spare in case either of the others breaks down. At work it means there's no stopping to make a single cup. And at dinner parties, it's working while, at last, you can relax. No one can possibly enjoy their own dinner parties much until the pudding is served. After that, though, being surrounded by people you're fond of who are enjoying your hospitality is wonderful.

The working lunch is one of the world's most over-rated meals. The business lunch is work in 'treats' clothing, but doesn't offer much value for money and in this country isn't tax-efficient unless you can blame it on a foreigner. Nobody in their right mind can seriously expect to do business on the basis of meeting their companion with a sherry, half a bottle of white wine, tomato soup, half a bottle of red wine, three ounces of beef in gravy, four ounces of peas, three ounces of potatoes mashed, roasted or chips, apples in a juice, custard (made with powder, in all but a handful of restaurants), a brandy, two coffees and a cigar. The one to benefit most from this is the secretary, who that afternoon has to do very little work, and won't need to run very fast.

Lunch can be enjoyable. Note for advertising people: a bit of fish boiled in a bag, even in a spotless formica-clad kitchen with or without clean children and your best mate – is no treat. The simplest fresh salad with a baked potato to warm you on the prettiest plate you've got, is. A really easy and delicious salad dressing is oil, vinegar, a splash of mustard and a pinch of sugar to taste! We're told eating at lunchtime is less fattening than at dinner time (though it's not the potato that's fattening, but the butter you're *not* going to put on it, that would be). Never eat standing up, or on the run, you don't feel satisfied. Anyway, I said this was to be a treat. A glass of wine with lunch is a treat. More than one isn't for most people, it's over-indulgence, you'll forget to fetch the children or, worse still, bring back the wrong ones, and you'll get no work done.

Here are a few recipe ideas worth passing on. For a starter there's the crudité dip, as served at one of my favourite London haunts, Eleven Park Walk. Then there are recipes which formed part of the light menu designed for the David Shilling week at the Grosvenor House Hotel, and finally the easiest chutney I know – and they're all deliciously good! If you happen to have vegetarian friends, they're perfect. There's a fresh asparagus salad garnished with blood oranges, a vegetable strudel as an alternative for colder days, a pudding made of rose petals, a dessert sauce.

Sauce for crudités

In a saucepan over a low heat, brown together olive oil, garlic and anchovies. Remove from heat, add chopped walnuts, salt and pepper and cream. Return to heat, and cook, stirring, till it's thick enough not to dribble off the crudités when they're dipped in. If possible, serve warm: if you haven't a table warmer or heated tray, improvise with nightlights...

Fresh asparagus salad

For each portion, you need mixed lettuces (radicchio, curly endive, oakleaf; 4 pieces lamb's lettuce); $\frac{1}{4}$ avocado, sliced; 4 sticks cooked asparagus; 4 segments blood orange; 1 tablespoon Hollandaise sauce, and 2 tablespoons dressing made with 1 tablespoon each olive and vegetable oil, and a dash each of soya sauce, truffle juice, lemon juice, salt and pepper.

Decorate the salad plate with all the lettuces except the lamb's lettuce, and sprinkle the dressing on. Arrange the sliced avocado on top, the lamb's lettuce leaves around the plate, with a segment of orange on each leaf. Place the still warm cooked asparagus tips (discard the stalks) on top of the avocados, and spoon the Hollandaise on.

Grosvenor House vegetable strudel

This makes ten portions: you need an onion, a clove of garlic, 200 grams each of carrots, leeks, celeriac, green beans, turnip (young white ones), and bean sprouts; 50 grams of butter; salt, pepper, nutmeg; 150 grams filo pastry. Cut the vegetables into fine strips and toss in butter; season well. Place them on top of the rolled-out filo pastry, and roll up like a Swiss roll. Bake for twenty minutes at 450°.

Rose petal flan

This is a sweet pastry base (4 oz sugar, 8 oz butter, 12 oz flour and an egg) lightly coated with rose-water flavoured creme patisserie (a pint of milk, 2 eggs, 4 oz sugar, 2 oz flour, ½ oz custard powder, rose water) and decorated with crystallized rose petals, preferably pink (dip petals in a solution of egg whites and lemon juice, then sprinkle with castor sugar). Serve it with a rose-water flavoured yogurt.

Easy dessert mint sauce

Lightly whip double cream with a little sugar, then add creme de menthe. When the Grosvenor House Hotel made this, they used a pint of cream, 2 ounces of sugar and ¼ pint of creme de menthe; you probably won't need so much. While the hotel served this with wonderful complicated chocolate mousses, I'd pour it over a good chocolate ice cream or even fresh fruit.

Gillian's Vale of Health one-minute chutney

Peel an apple and an orange, and put them with a green chili and an handful of green mint, a squeeze of lemon and salt to taste in the blender.

The easiest food treat in the summer is the picnic; all you really need is cheese, bread and your favourite drink; throw them into a bag with a large tablecloth or rug for sitting on and set out. You don't have to drive out to the sea or the country – why not take your simple picnic in a paved area, to the cinema, to a park, or on a train going nowhere in particular? Take an extrovert picnic on a bus. Have a Sunday brunch picnic with cereals (and milk and sugar), orange juice, and croissants and jam... (No picnic I've been to yet is as exotic as that in the most famous painting of a picnic, 'Déjeuner sur l'herbe', with reclining nudes – now there's a thought for the ambitious picnic-maker.)

If you are planning something adventurous, make contingency plans against the weather, even if this only means clearing space in your living room to set down a rug. Sitting on the floor gives the atmosphere of novelty, bonhomie is enhanced by the pitter-patter of tiny hailstones on the window-pane! There is no limit to how grandly you can prepare your picnic.

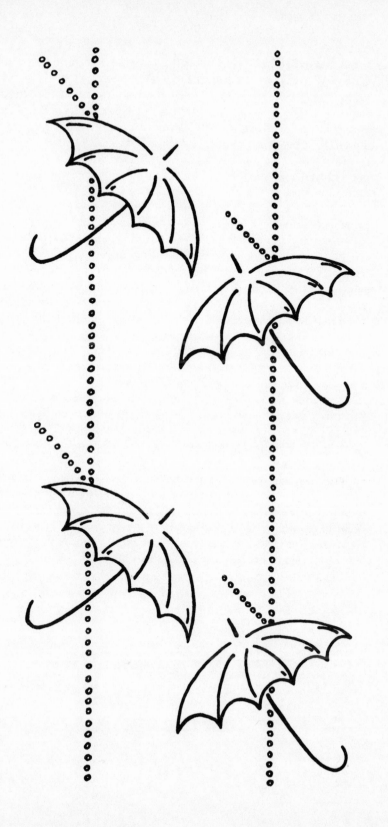

The most luxurious picnics are still being carried on in the manner of Queen Victoria, with full staff accompaniment. After all, it's England and it could rain – so why *not* take an umbrella and a holder with you? Especially if he's also going to help set up your chairs and a table. (Is it true that cocktails went out of fashion when people could no longer afford to keep employing a cocktail shaker? A friend's husband recently teased her that if only she was better in the kitchen, they could get rid of the cook. She replied that if only he was better in the bedroom, they could also get rid of the chauffeur.)

In the Royal Enclosure car park at Ascot during the week, I've seen parties of eight or more seated for picnics beside the car, although there are adequate restaurant facilities. During a short sharp shower they ate off family china with staff holding umbrellas over them. One friend's picnic was ruined by a downpour so strong they swear the salmon swam off the serving platter, and all their food ended up on the grass. Luckily, wine bottles are more resilient and the odd drop of rainwater in champagne seems to do little to upset anyone's appetite for it.

If you haven't a car park space arranged beforehand, the train is more convenient for travelling because you avoid the dreadful traffic jams that build up even before midday – and the station is only a five-minute walk from the course. Unless you applied for your Royal Enclosure Badge vouchers at the beginning of the year, you'll only be able to buy a badge to get into the public enclosures; if you want to go spotting the rich and famous make for the Paddock between races. If you've been invited to a box, then it's all too easy to let the day drift by without moving from there because you'll be waited on hand and foot. (The boxes are not very spacious, so some hosts employ the service of their favourite interior designer to spoil their quarters even more.) A lot of people think the only way to arrive at Ascot is by helicopter, although you land further away than the station. If you're going by helicopter, hang on to your hat on leaving!

Fashionable summer picnics feature S and S, salmon and strawberries, whether as tinned salmon sandwiches and strawberry ice-
cream, or a whole fish with salads and something delicious with the
berries. My own Ascot first-day picnic avoided this duo. I hadn't
planned it till the night before, so I bought vine-leaves and stuffed
them myself with spoonfuls of rice, cooked with a little onion, a few
spices, herbs and black pepper. The most time-consuming part was
spooning the rice on to the leaves and making the parcels – but they
were clean and easy to eat, and tasted excellent with the champagne. I
bought a crisp lettuce, cut good carrots into strips, and served these
with a quiche (fry some onions, add some lightly grilled tomatoes,
and/or mushrooms, a couple of eggs, some milk and stir into pastry
case and bake in the oven). I also prepared a speedy cake (wholemeal
flour, a couple of eggs, a small lump of butter, sugar, mixed dried
fruits, desiccated coconut and ground almonds all mixed together,
then baked). You'll have gathered that I think cooking can be simple;
with my methods it is fun and full of interest – and the experiments
often produce delicious new dishes. I don't even own scales as I feel
they're a waste of my time, and a curb to inventiveness.

The most important part of my preparations were in the packing. I
used a hat box 13½ inches square, covered in pretty paper (actually,
one of my wallpapers). The cake went in first, and all the foods were
wrapped in silver foil. Everything else – glasses, crockery (my
'Interlude' china by Coalport – complete with ashtrays) – was
wrapped in bright pink tissue, echoing the colour of the pattern on the
china. I put in a couple of extra glasses and plates just in case more
friends turned up (of course, they did) and a small vase for flowers. I
used a couple of sprays of carnations – just as right for this picnic as
some of the amazing table centres I saw. I also packed real serviettes,
which match the china, and a large table cloth. There was a plastic bag
for waste and mess, though I'd deliberately chosen foods that wouldn't
make much: no sauces, or salads with dressings, or strawberries and
cream. Finally, I put in champagne, and iced coffee in a Thermos,
already mixed with a little sugar. I also took a bottle of mineral water,
but on this occasion only the flowers drank it.

This simple outline could be adapted to suit anyone's pocket or
taste: add crisps, olives, cherries, cold meats, bread already buttered –
even take 'six-packs' instead of champagne. (In fact, my pink Piper-
Heidseick came in packs of six, giving a fresh slant to that phrase.)

The quintessential Ascot picnic is that given by the Honourable Mrs
Patrick Penny to her lucky guests. Over several years she's perfected
her formula so that now it hardly changes year to year, to the delight of

her friends. The food is set out on a professional paper-hanger's table, because it's long and thin, and easy and practical to erect. Guests serve themselves: her cold salmon is dressed in aspic and garnished with giant Pacific prawns and thinly-sliced cucumber. The picnic is always early in Ascot week, when salmon is still a treat, but she offers alternatives: there are devilled eggs (hardboiled, with the yolks finely sieved with mayonnaise mixed with Tabasco and Lee & Perrins, then piped back in) and lobster. Because her fishmonger is closed on Mondays, she keeps them alive over the weekend in the bath (her house has a spare bathroom!). She used to keep them in a sink, but one year they escaped; ice cubes help keep them drowsy. Each portion is half of a lobster weighing between three quarters and one pound. There are hot new potatoes sprinkled with chopped fresh parsley; these travel to Ascot in a Thermos. Experience has shown that food put into a Thermos piping hot will go on cooking; potatoes will sweat; let things cool a little first. There is a Hollandaise sauce to pour over the potatoes; it travels in a separate container, but the best plan is to put this into a huge Thermos with the potatoes, which will give enough steam to keep the sauce perfect. It is the first thing unpacked and checked. If it's separated because it was too hot, the remedy is to throw in one ice cube and whisk briskly with a fork until it re-forms. In another Thermos are hot garden peas with mint.

There is also a large bowl of shrimp cocktail, simply made with mayonnaise, Heinz ketchup, Worcester sauce and Tabasco, and a squeeze of lemon, with cayenne pepper sprinkled on top for colour.

Her amazing salad usually consists of lettuce, with apples, Cheddar cheese, black and white grapes halved and seeded, very finely sliced red and green peppers, spring onions; at the last minute, before leaving home, she adds cubes of blue cheese and finally avocado. This has to be added at the last minute, otherwise it goes to a black mush. This salad is served with a scintillating French dressing.

Now for the puddings! Thinking of tea later, Mrs Penny warns that you shouldn't over-cater: girls just pick, and chaps only want extra blotter so they can consume more drink. Nevertheless, she always serves raspberries because in mid-June they're only just available, and they are carefully ordered from New Covent Garden Market and she serves them in a large bowl with double cream and sugar from an antique silver sifter.

Champagne is the order of the day, chilled, either plain or with a little framboise and a raspberry floating on top.

Henley is a great outdoor social occasion, the atmosphere is calmer than at Ascot (perhaps it's the effect of being at the water's edge?). The races are continuous throughout the day, and Henley isn't yet the fashion parade that Ascot is. Though it's becoming more dressy, it also offers a chance for men to do their thing. In 1985 a black-leather-clad couple arrived by motorbike, so avoiding the dreadful traffic jams that build up quite early. They changed into more formal wear in the car park, and their sense of fun earned them a round of applause from a cluster of older ladies. (Two tips for Henley: take gumboots, and get organized in April.) A salad I've been served on a Henley picnic was interestingly different: Mrs Ward covers a head of celery, sliced, mixed with a head of lettuce, with slices of avocado; sprinkles caster sugar over this, then lemon juice, single cream and finally a little hot water. (No salt, no pepper.) This goes very well with salmon en croute.

Henley car park has a more relaxed atmosphere than Ascot's, but if anything the picnics have even more formality. More tables are prettily laid out in great style, the flower arrangements toning perfectly with the tablecloths, chairs and garden umbrellas. Of course the food is appropriately festive! One enterprising Henley picnicker makes their whole salmon different by arranging it like a boat, with asparagus for oars and shrimps for oarsmen.

The lawns at Glyndebourne offer a marvellous setting for a picnic. Formally – rather than spectacularly-dressed diners eschew the very good restaurants to picnic – although of course the weather is unpredictable. It's only worth picnicking here if you're really going to make an effort, but there's still a certain 'one-upmanship' for those who do.

John Cox of the Scottish Opera maintains that the chief challenge of the Glyndebourne picnic is that you have to commit yourself to it before you know what the weather will be like. If, at eleven o'clock, it looks as though rain has set in for the day you'll still have to go ahead with it – there's little chance of getting a table in the restaurant. Everything should be easy to eat in the car (no paper plates, nothing that needs strenuous cutting). There is a highly refined car-picnic fraternity: no jostling for places by the lake (midges), the ha-ha (cows), or the marquee (people). When the late Robin Maugham gave a picnic, his chauffeur took off his cap, exchanged his black leather driving gloves for white cotton ones, let down the back of the vintage Bentley to form a convenient serving table, lit the candelabra as he saw Robin and his party enter the car park during the interval, and handed out champagne in gilded beakers.

If you intend to sit on the ground, you have to beware of sharing your picnic with dogs and ducks (indeed, moorhens). The current production of *Figaro* has three intervals, and picnickers like to eat a course in each. John has a story of two Tibetan spaniels, Gisella of Curwenna and Kenley Kublai Khan, working their way through a fresh cream dessert and starting on the Stilton during Act III.

Tables came to Glyndebourne with *The Rake's Progress* which David Hockney designed in 1975, bringing his own particular jeunesse dorée to a first night not entirely typical of the Glyndebourne scene. All these people were to be brought in by private coach and fed (by Peter Langan). John realized something serious was afoot when he was asked to a picnic rehearsal one lunchtime. On the night, an astonished audience merged for the interval to see tables the length of the ha-ha, deeply clothed in white samite and staffed by more Latin American waiters than you could use in the chorus of *The Barber of Seville*. The food and the wine were provided in such quantities that the entire opera company, chorus and orchestra were bidden to eat up the remains after the show was over. As mist and darkness simultaneously fell, candles guttered and the stage electricians brushed the scene with tactful spotlights.

Of course, one man's treat is another man's poison. We all love ending a meal by diving into a box of chocolates – great, unless you're grossly overweight and need to compensate by diving into a swimming pool (but don't, because you don't want anyone to see your body) or jogging. This *may* be some people's idea of a good time – the winds whistling in your ears, the coarse feel of concrete paving underfoot – but I feel that, in an age where swearing no longer causes surprise even on children's television, 'Go forth and jog' would be a worse obscenity to me than 'Go forth and multiply.'

Drinks

These three were served during the David Shilling week at Grosvenor House – they are named after hats in my 1986 Summer Collection

In the Pink

$\frac{1}{6}$ oz orange curaçao, 1 oz fresh strawberry puree, topped with champagne

Double Vision

Champagne laced with $\frac{1}{6}$ oz creme de banane, topped with $\frac{1}{6}$ oz Southern Comfort

Head in the Clouds

1 oz guava juice topped with champagne; add 1 oz poire William and small particles of gold leaf

Long Island Iced Tea

Tequila, vodka, gin, rum, Coke, lemon juice; crushed ice

Bistro Garden Long Island Iced Tea

Brandy, rum, gin, vodka, dry vermouth, Sweet'N Sour;
crushed ice; top up with Coke in a long glass

Cape Cod

Cranberry juice, vodka; crushed ice

Harry Cipriani's Bellini

Two-thirds fresh peach juice, one-third Italian
champagne

Mouton New Year's Day Tea

To China tea add a little honey, lemon and a dash of
whisky

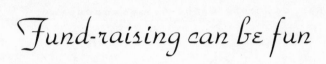 Fund-raising can be fun

The most exhilarating fund-raising event I've taken part in was the Night of A Hundred Stars at the Theatre Royal, Drury Lane. When I was asked, I wasn't going to let a little thing like the fact that I had never ever been on the stage before – no, not even at school, I promise you – stop me from trying this time. Yes, I said, I'd love to do it. And then a few doubts set in. Everyone kept telling me how enormous the stage of the Theatre Royal is – I was just worried that I couldn't sing – well, I never had before – and that being a designer I'd have to wear something pretty special!

Luckily there was a 'press call' organized at the theatre, and as a host of stars (including lots of friends who gave me encouragement, such as Joanna Lumley and Sian Phillips) sipped their drinks and did interviews, I slipped away on to the stage of the Theatre Royal. So many people had warned me how huge I'd find the stage, that it was vast, that I was prepared to be overawed by it, and however much I knew I wanted the experience of doing my solo on the stage of the Theatre Royal, Drury Lane – after all, not many people have started off at that prestigious address, most people dream of ending up there! I was prepared to give up if I didn't feel happy about doing it. But do you know, the minute I was on the stage it felt good – just like entering a large, but certainly not vast, empty drawing room where a party was due to be held and the furniture had yet to arrive – but in time you knew it would all happen. I paced across the open stage, counting how many strides I needed to get from one side to the other and then measured from front to back in the same way. I looked out at the empty Stalls, up to the beautiful boxes and then at the Circle and Upper Circle. Already I felt elation, exhilaration, and knew that if I worked at it my introduction to the Theatre would be the experience of a lifetime. I was going to enjoy that experience – even if the audience didn't! I practised with the choreographers and over the next two or three weeks at every opportunity I'd turn on my cassette recorder, clear the floor of the shop, and do mini rehearsals. On the day of the dress rehearsal I was pretty nervous – I'd never sung accompanied by a live pianist before – you couldn't just put him on pause like the recorder. This was the real thing. At the end of the piece I ran through, finding the words just in the dark of my memory. I leapt off into the wings and there was silence as the music ended. 'You've forgotten to play my encore music,' I came back on and shouted at the pianist – more perhaps from panic than inflated ego, but in the stalls Jack Tinker, the *Daily Mail*'s drama critic, and Joan Plowright howled in amazement. The only amateur, I was the only one who'd taken for granted that I would have music for my reprise!

In the shared dressing rooms there were great joviality and camaraderie, but as the time for the opening approached an exhilarating tension mounted. And then we were told that Their Royal Highnesses, the Duke and Duchess of Gloucester were attending and we would have to bow to the Royal Box when we all went on stage for the opening number, 'Another Opening of Another Show'. That went off OK – I was on fairly early in the evening so just had to follow the performers in front of me, as the stars kept appearing: Judi Dench, Colin Blakely, Oliver Tobias, Joss Ackland – all real pros. I changed and got back to the wings, took my position behind the curtains at the top of the staircase I had to make my entrance on – not just my first time on stage but a solo entrance down a staircase to centre stage as well. I'm a lucky guy. Suddenly everyone had finished singing their song and I heard my music start to play – adrenalin rushed to all the right places – I blew my whistle – and I was away – I wore an Edwardian child's sailor suit – with shorts, neat white socks, shoes with straps, a sailor top with the collar in navy and white and a huge round straw hat on the back of my head, and as I skipped childishly to the centre of the stage I started to sing 'On the go-oo-ood ship – Loioll-i-pop' and if that didn't bring the house down the way I leapt across the stage throwing sweets for the second chorus, imitating the sort of exaggerated movements that child stars made at the turn of the century managed to get almost everyone laughing – and I needed that music to get me back for my encore!

It was one of the most exhilarating experiences of my life, but as I made my way back to the dressing room I was relieved it was all over and felt apprehension for those who still had to go on. At the end of the show we all had to go on stage and sing 'It's Not How You Start, It's How You Finish', and as I was lined up next to Sir Michael Hordern and Christopher Reeve I felt if I'm never asked to perform again it was one hell of a stage career! The evening raised over £15,000 for the Spina Bifida Association.

There had been a minor crisis which could have turned into disaster during the afternoon but was averted by quick thinking, and action, and the generosity of Simon Callow. I got into my costume well before time and went to the back of the theatre where they were serving light refreshments, learning my words all the way – I thought I'd never be able to remember them. I suddenly looked up and there was Simon, also dressed in shorts and sailor top and a little flabbergasted. He was going to be singing 'Sonny Boy', sitting on Frank Finlay's knee and although I couldn't do 'Good Ship' in anything but a 'sailor boy' outfit he said he'd be willing to change: how could we? Well, I'm a designer aren't I? I dashed into my car to pick up a schoolboy costume – my home is only ten minutes away – or was that day! I don't dress up my girlfriends as schoolboys for orgies – but striped blazers had been the fashion a couple of years ago, and as you'll find out I seldom throw good clothes away. I also had a good selection of striped ties! This outfit was so successful that I got a phone-call a few months later to borrow the blazer again, this time for the Royal Variety Show.

My singing career did not end at that one performance. I went on to sing at the Dominion Theatre in front of the Duchess of Kent, in an event to raise money for Unicef. It was another star-studded lineup that included Nigel Hawthorne, Charles Dance, Charlton Heston, Diane Keen and Richard O'Brien, and I sang 'Who Wants To Be A Milliner'.

I've only been into a recording studio once, and that was to make 'You'll Never Walk Alone' in aid of the Bradford City Disaster Fund. At first my friends laughed at the idea of my being on a record, but they stopped when it was Number One in the British charts for several weeks in 1985. I can honestly say, though, that this success has not changed me, although I do find I now quite often wear a scarf in winter to protect myself – just like real singers do!

Around the world, museums and art galleries have charity committees to raise money, called variously 'Patrons' or 'Friends of...'. You can join these groups for a very small membership fee, although they may hope for large donations or hard-working members too. The benefits include invitations to special events, private viewings of exhibitions, some organize tours of living artists' studios, or to houses of historic interest, or lectures. Most arrange for their galleries to be open at special times for the uninterrupted enjoyment of their members.

If you'd like to raise money for a favourite charity, you've first got to think of a scheme. Bob Geldof and Ian Botham in their very different ways have reminded us that we can each one of us raise money to benefit others less fortunate than ourselves. There are plenty of ways you can do this. Some of the ways may be more self-indulgent than others, but the ends would seem to justify the means. Some events, such as organizing a disco or a jumble sale, appeal less to people's charitable instincts than their desire for a good night out, or a bargain, or both!

Fashion shows are really hard to organize but if you ask friends to model, you're sure that their relations and friends will take tickets. It shouldn't be hard to get the help not just of a local store or fashion shop, but also ask a local hairdresser to do the hair, a beauty shop to do the make-up. (Go to other shops for other events, and get them to donate prizes for a raffle, or ask them to publicize the event by telling their customers or putting up a poster even, if it and the event are suited to the clientele.)

Always prepare well in advance for each eventuality. Get someone, perhaps the local disco, to supply not just the music but the lighting also – and try to get all these things donated – that is, for free. On the day, get everyone to arrive on a strict schedule. If you think they'll be late, schedule them a bit early, but you don't want too many people scurrying around doing nothing long before the event begins – they'll just get fidgety and bored. For fashion shows beginning about midday, the first models arrive for professional make-up around seven o'clock in the morning.

In 1986 I showed my hats at a fashion show and dinner at Woburn Abbey, honoured by the presence of Princess Anne and Captain Mark Phillips, to which many guests had come from fair distances to support the Horse Trials Support Group and the Save the Children Fund; they included many celebrities from the horsey world, and half were people living locally. The Marquis and Marchioness of Tavistock belonged to both groups.

Truly it seemed that every one of the 250 guests had a great time, and this was due mainly to the fact that they all wanted to. It was a magnificent venue, of course.

In the dining room the catwalk was situated down the middle, and planted down either side were prettily appointed dining tables with yellow and white flowers arranged as small trees in the centre of each table. The room had Romanesque temple-like columns and arches each end and interesting pictures featuring many Dukes and Duchesses of Bedford. Champagne flowed from the start of the reception till after dinner when a Balthazar bottle was auctioned for £700. Her Royal Highness looked stunning in a black velvet suit with a neat white mink collar to flatter the face, and the Marchioness of Tavistock wore a soft cocktail dress in a stunning purple silk. The men looked formally smart in black ties. But essentially this was a local affair, with local catering, local hairdressers, local make-up, some local professional models (models from the horsey world included Lucinda and David Greene, Virginia Long and Emma Wilkinson), and it was a local shop who supplied all the clothes. It raised a lot of money as well as raising a lot of spirits. Although I always warn people who intend to put on a fashion show to raise money for charity that an enormous amount of work is involved, it proves that it can be done and done successfully.

I also showed some of my hats at a charity fashion show organized by Princess George Galitzine for PHAB (the Physically Handicapped and Able Bodied association), which was honoured by the presence of the

Duchess of Gloucester. She arrived looking stunning in a fitted white jacket, with huge black polka dots, and a narrow black skirt. I've often thought it a disadvantage to bear the initial 'S' because in alphabetical order one comes so far down the list, but here it meant that out of eleven designers my name came one from the last. A couple of days before the event I was asked whether I minded having my hats modelled by dancers from the London Contemporary Dance Theatre rather than models, because the professionals needed extra time to change for the final number. I said I didn't; although I have always believed in trying different staging for a fashion show, I'd never used a group of dancers before.

In the end, the eight girls and two men brought more applause from the audience than any of the models. They all wore black leotards. I'd chosen some music from *Chicago*, the musical, the first piece being romantic for four girls wearing the sophisticated hats, supported by the boys modelling my men's jackets, then the tempo changed with the music 'Jail House Tango', a wild and witty song about Chicago murderesses of the Thirties, and the second four girls showed some wild 'show-stopping' hats – and managed to highstep over the boys who did cartwheels around them.

There are lots of other ways to raise money apart from putting on fashion shows. In daily order, coffee mornings, lunches, teas, drinks parties or dinners, all provide opportunities. You can put on all sorts of contests, even the corny holiday-camp-type ones – spaghetti-eating contests, glamorous grannies, knobbly knees. How about a card evening, or mock race meeting? Perhaps a show at a local sports club, a tennis tournament, a cricket match, an exhibition of art. All these and masses of others could be used as vehicles to raise funds – probably with accompanying spin-offs like a raffle, tombola, a programme where you can sell advertising space – and if you invite a local photographer to take photographs these could be sold to the guests if they want them with some financial arrangement made with the photographer before-hand for the charity to benefit.

It's a great help if you can use local talent, whether it's footballers or painters – their relatives and friends are bound to support them. You may not think that people you know are that talented, but ask around. You may find you've enough enthusiasm even to put on a show. You might even have a celebrity or two you could call on.

Of course there are ways of raising funds all on your own. Getting people to sponsor you doing something crazy or even mildly dangerous are two of the most obvious ways. What is your particular talent? I once did a sponsored 'stopping nail biting' and lasted several weeks! There are many schemes that anyone can carry out, and local radio

Revlon

Yellow and black lacquered straw with polka dots, worn by Michelle and photographed by Alistair Hughes

Two totally different approaches to looking stunning: (*above*) Lesley Anne
Down in a cream straw hat with silk flowers and veiling, photographed by Sir
Cecil Beaton, and (*opposite*) Raquel Welch, wearing a black silk hat with bows
and veiling, photographed by Clive Arrowsmith

Hanger hat in black velvet and gold/silver striped lamé, worn by Annabel
Heseltine and photographed by Alistair Hughes

and newspapers are often very interested and keen to help.

You could get people to sponsor your giving up smoking – that would help you and the charity – or sponsor a sensible weight-reducing programme. A walk, a run, a marathon swim, are other ideas – and there are masses of oddball schemes, too. If you approach your local radio and newspaper you might find you can enlist their help. They'll obviously need a story out of it, so you're likely to do best if you can explain why you think the charity is so worth while – or if your scheme is slightly oddball. Most of us can walk four miles, not a lot of us can cross the English Channel in a beer barrel, living only off Cheddar cheese. (Something like this should get sponsorship from a brewery and the cheese marketing board.) More seriously, though, funds don't just need to be raised for existing charities; if you see what you feel is an injustice, it's time to raise some money to right that wrong.

Raise large sums of money by setting up committees – it certainly makes raising the funds a less lonely job. You'll need a committee if you want to run a fashion show. Some people feel that the more members of a committee you have the easier it will be, especially if you have some prestigious members. Of course you want their help, but what you really want is people who'll really do some work – both selling tickets and helping with preparation before and on the night. If people are working on the night, you can't expect them to buy tickets for themselves too. If you're going to have a brochure with advertising or a tombola you can elect small sub-committees of maybe no more than three or four which can then concentrate on this particular task and be responsible for it. A similar principle applies with the main committee – about twelve will feel really committed. If there are fifty on the committee many will feel 'Let the others work hard.' Of course, the Chairman and Secretary have to be prepared to do the most work, and you should have a Treasurer in charge of the money.

A small committee I was on with Annabel Heseltine, Lady Helen Windsor, Dr Mark Cecil, and no more than a dozen others, managed to fill the Hippodrome in London for a disco and so make a substantial contribution to the Sharon Allen Leukaemia Fund. And 1,500 guests had a lot of fun.

I swam recently in a charity race. Angharad Rees phoned me and asked me to be in Chris Cazenove's team. Nothing strenuous she said – you can float about on a raft if you like. To me swimming is best done in the sunshine beside a sunbed complete with long refreshing drink, maybe with an amusing book open but probably not read – and the swimming part is to refresh you from time to time and also improve the tan. Imagine my surprise when I found I was swimming against Duncan Goodhew! He won.

Another time I was asked to race for charity was in a celebrity race at Kempton Park. This sounded a wonderful opportunity – even though Mark Burns, who'd been in *Chariots of Fire*, was in it. I pictured myself in some dashing racing silks – at six foot tall, it might have a bit of a squeeze, but I was sure we'd manage somehow. It was unnecessary, though. The race was on donkeys – and highly undignified. My donkey started off all right – and in the right direction – and we went rather well, but a couple of feet from the finishing post it decided to stop and would move no further. Of course Mark Burns won, but then everyone else went past us, and still my donkey wouldn't budge. The crowd – which was quite large, not because of our 'classic' race but because this was part of a busy bank holiday meeting – roared encouragement until finally the animal shot over the line. Now I know what's meant by getting the last laugh.

 # Parties

$\mathcal{A}$ friend of mine claims he went to a party for the Kentucky Derby, given by a racehorse breeder who chose an Egyptian theme, and ended up by buying four camels and an elephant to complete the picture because it was cheaper to buy them, than to hire them. Rivalling even this extravagance is the sort of party where guests are literally flown in for the occasion – but I'm not quite sure one member of the racing fraternity had got it quite right for his birthday celebration. All right, he'd booked ten hotels for his nine hundred guests to stay overnight, and he'd arranged to charter enough planes to get them there. On the invitations he gave hours of times for the planes, adding that if you wanted to arrange your own private plane here was the telephone number to ring – but if you took the charter planes you had to pay £75 a seat! It reminds us that, however rich, everyone's always on some kind of budget.

I suppose one of the reasons people enjoy my parties – it can't be the extravagance! – is that they're likely to meet such a variety of people. We all know that if you get a group of accountants together, they'll only talk figures (but can you believe some of them?) but mix them up and you'll have much more fun. Rock stars love meeting Duchesses, whatever they'd have you believe, and actors just love, well frankly, the opportunity to be seen. Most models don't say much – which is probably all the better for all concerned. Politicians, of course, have lots to say: but if it gets too heavy-going you could always try ringing a bell. They might be absent-minded enough to nip off back to the House!

There is only one reason to give a party: FUN. Don't give a party if you feel you owe a few people a return of their hospitality – that attitude's bound to end in a disastrous evening. Usually there's a reason to give a party, big or small, a wedding, a birthday, an anniversary. If not, invent a reason – a celebration for a friend, your mother's birthday, no better reason than it's Tuesday! Giving parties is good for you, and for your friends if it's done right.

For a dinner party, the ambience is as important as the food and drink. I use careful lighting in my dining room, and take great pains over laying the table so that when guests enter they are immediately presented with a feast for the eye. I don't know whether it was this that prompted Wedgwood to ask me to set a table using their white and gold 'Florentine' pattern – they wanted it photographed by Fritz von Schulenberg (you may have seen it in *House & Garden* magazine) as part of a promotion in Selfridges.

First I did a sketch of what I wanted the photograph to show; I decided on a table set for a romantic meal for two couples. Flowers were ordered, tablecloths chosen and arranged – I took even longer than I would for one of my own dinner parties. I went round Selfridges' Food Hall (the studio where we were working was nearby) choosing a rich mixture of perfectly toning chocolates to fill one bowl, of pretzels and cashews for another. Most people choosing food look for interesting tastes – although I kept that in mind, appearances were absolutely vital. I'd asked for gold cutlery, to go with the gold of the pattern on the dinner service. At first this didn't arrive, as Selfridges thought it was too valuable to send over for a photographic session. Finally, amidst great security, four gold place settings arrived – and the photography went ahead.

So much effort had gone into this that Selfridges decided to show the actual table setting (and those done by other designers) in the store. I feared they wouldn't be able to recreate it – but they did. When I went to see, there was every pale green grape in place, every gold-foil wrapped Belgian chocolate just as I would have wanted, just the right lighting to enhance the overall evening atmosphere. Again, the gold cutlery caused the only problem. It was there, all right, but every night it had to be taken away by security men and every morning put back in position. Incredibly, not one piece was stolen; not even a pretzel taken.

I don't suggest you should go to quite these lengths for a dinner party, but I do recommend you get yourself organized well in advance. In a large well-run household, guests arriving early don't pose a problem. But even if you haven't got staff, don't panic. Welcome the guests politely, steer them firmly into the drawing room (keep them well away from the kitchen even when they offer, unless you know they'll be able to help – personally, I'd suspect the abilities of anyone who turned up early). Give them a drink, or ask them to help themselves. Wine (or fruit juice or mineral water) is easiest – don't offer complicated cocktails. Sit them down, and if there's a magazine handy give it to them – don't worry at this point about its contents – and get on with what you still have to do.

People do turn up early, as well as late, so try to have everything ready at least five or ten minutes before your first guests are due. If you're nervous before your parties, you'll still find some last-minute thing to do to fill in those few minutes.

Give little gifts at dinner parties; it helps to know your guests pretty well, and you don't have to be Rockefeller. Recently I've served little chocolate mice with the coffee at the end of the meal, and quickly realized I should buy extras for people to take home. Because I've a terrific fish and chip shop near me, and some American friends were longing to have a meal of real English fish and chips, they had their wish - and I found some cheap pens made in the shape of a fish and a chip, in plastic, and gave them these as mementos of what otherwise proved for me an inexpensive and (best of all) effortless meal. Instead of the traditional flower arrangement you could always place a rose, say, across each dinner plate; or a rose for each female guest and a carnation for the men.

As a guest at an informal party a few flowers, chocolates, a bottle of wine, just an amusing little keepsake, make an appropriate sign of gratitude for being invited; I feel strongly that you should always thank after a party either by letter or telephone and certainly within 48 hours. It doesn't have to be a long letter - an amusing or whimsical postcard with an appropriate line or two does the trick if your host or you are too busy to get to the phone - but if you've ever given a series of parties you'll know how frustrating it is if certain people never show their appreciation of you with a brief note. Sending a bouquet of flowers is always a charming alternative but more expensive. Try to sign the card yourself, by asking the florist to fetch it if you have telephoned your order. This is not instead of thanking as you leave which, unless you are wildly drunk, you should always do (you should never ever get that drunk!) Or it might also be that your host is in an embarrassing position too!

Try your best to thank him/her anyway, trying to ignore his/her incapacity and make your exit swiftly (especially if you feel the cops might be on their way!) I've noticed a habit recently of the young and rich to find themselves in couples or groups underneath tables with starched white linen tablecloths for camouflage at even the most grand gatherings and long before the party's due to end. If you're looking for someone and see a table appear to move you may have located your quarry, but I suggest it is generally an inappropriate time to interrupt.

At some formal gatherings, guests may be announced on their arrival to their hosts - all the guest must do is, when asked, give his or her name to the person who announces it. Speak as clearly as possible and on hearing your name step forward to be greeted. In say, a wedding, you may be meeting your host or their family for the first time - don't worry, it's not a time for deep conversation. 'How nice to be here,' or something similar, will be sufficient. If there is a long queue of people to be introduced, it would be impolite to say much more, so just add 'I do hope we have the chance to meet later.' The same formula can be used when you are the host. 'How nice to see you', 'How good of you to come' breaks the ice sufficiently. When you are the host it is perhaps harder to remember that there may be more guests waiting to be introduced and get down to what they really came for, that is, enjoying the party, so you too must keep your chats brief.

I was recently introduced at a grand party, and as the hostess got around to mentioning my name, I realized I was the only man present who didn't bear the name of an important piece of land in Britain. No titles were mentioned but David Shilling stuck out like the proverbial sore thumb.

At all parties, introduce people to each other. It is not much help in breaking the ice if you just tell two people each other's names. Try to think up a simple line or two when you're introducing two people, that will intrigue the one without offending the other, and set the ball in motion. A host must constantly be working at his/her own party, and that doesn't mean spending all your time in the kitchen. You should also be keeping an eye on how the conversation's cooking too.

It's a nice gesture for a host/hostess to greet their guests on arrival. But where they are neither opening the door of the home nor in a formal or informal line-up, a guest should try to locate them fairly soon after arrival. If you are stopped by other friends before doing so, this should be used as an excuse for cutting the conversation short – and you can always return to those friends later.

The success of the party is very much up to the participants. You can make a simple evening into a party. A few candles, something pleasant to drink, a little care with your decoration, and you've set the romantic mood for the party and a special evening even if it's only two of you – or perhaps especially so!

Holding a party is hard but satisfying work, and it can be fun. If you're too busy, and rich enough, you can hire someone to do all the work for you. Lady Elizabeth Anson is the English doyenne of Partyplanners, and often runs several a day from the nerve-centre in the basement of her home in Ladbroke Grove, complete with computer, constantly-busy telephones and a large staff. If you're a special client, she'll discuss the plans with you in her drawing room, and a very few sip champagne in the cool of her study, amidst her collection of 295 replica eggs.

If there's a specific reason for the party you've got a theme. If not, invent one. First decide who you want to invite, and who honestly will be able to come. These may be very different! And give yourself enough time to plan the party. Don't use party-giving simply as a means of social climbing. The more you give selflessly and plan the party for your guests, the more likely you are to have a success. You give a party in the hope that return invitations will flow in, naturally, but this isn't the raison d'être. So when you've got your guest list together, think how you can best keep them amused and what those guests will most enjoy. Older people don't like terribly loud music, most young people do. Old people need seating and some people simply prefer it; but then it is harder to keep the party moving. A little music on softly in the background when guests are first arriving helps create an atmosphere and is one of the first ways for you to set the mood you like from calm to frenzy. You are in control of each and every one of your guests from the moment they step through your front door. In fact even before, probably. However large or small the party, however social or shy we are, we all make some preparations before a party – whether it's buying a new outfit or simply trying to ascertain who we'll know who's going to be there, or who won't be there.

Before you get as far as inviting the first person, you must work out what form you want your party to take. If you've left one or two names off your guest list, think how hurt those people may be not to be invited. (They may of course be relieved – but we're going to make sure this party of yours actually works!) A friend I invited to a large drinks party didn't turn up – and then I saw him later that evening in a restaurant. My next party was a smaller, select affair, to which he wasn't invited. He was deeply shocked and hurt but I'd the perfect excuse: 'I didn't invite you because when I did, you didn't turn up – so I guessed if you weren't invited, you would.'

Phone calls are not always the easiest way to invite your friends to a party, though you are likely to get an instant answer. However small your numbers it is worth keeping a written invitation list. The easiest way is just to write all the names of those you intend to invite and the phone numbers (put work and home numbers down, but note which is which) and then jot a brief note by their names: yes/no, no reply – left message on answering machine. Expect to have to follow up message if you don't get a reply – answering machines aren't always reliable, nor are room-mates/flat-mates, parents etc... You can expect secretaries and husbands and wives to be – unless proved otherwise previously.

If you've given parties in the past that haven't been the greatest success, be honest with yourself and ask yourself why. Be brave and profit by your mistakes.

Frequent causes of failure

1. Lack of drink.
2. Too much drink (yes, it is possible!).
3. Police breaking up the party because of neighbours' complaints. (Is it easier to ask them, will they not come anyhow).
4. A badly thought out guest list.
5. Arranging your party to clash with another – or Dynasty!

There are certain questions you must ask yourself before you start giving invitations:

When do you want your guests to arrive? Stress promptness if you are preparing food that needs them at a special time – you could even be planning a trip to the theatre or opera. Tell them if you expect them promptly.

Do you want them to wear anything special? From black tie to fancy dress?

Do you want them to bring friends, only if they ask to, or definitely not at all?

Do you need them to bring, say, wine or food; the effort of a dinner party can be shared if friends bring the desserts or even every course, or is this expecting too much of them? And is it likely to be a gourmet disaster, not because of the quality of the food but the mixture of the menu, if you don't collate it. Can you control what they bring? Perhaps there's a dish a friend served which you particularly liked? Why not suggest it? And it's flattering.

It is essential to stress where you want them, and make sure they write the exact address down unless they are frequent visitors to your home – and especially if it's not at your home. You might suggest or enquire as to their modes of transport. If you really want people to attend, you can arrange lifts if you can face the added burden that entails. It seems sensible for as many of the party not to be driving as possible, but make sure that people who get lifts to the party know in advance whether or not they will also get a lift home. Also I can't emphasize enough giving directions. I always have to stress that I live in Blank Road, because there is also Blank Street running parallel – friends of mine from Australia, via Jersey, were in London for only a day. They waited for half an hour outside the wrong house one evening, thought they got the wrong night for the party, gave up and went home! Round the corner in Blank Road we were dancing till dawn. They'd just seen the name and had not checked whether it was Street or Road. The 'neighbours', sadly for me, never seem to be in, so they can't redirect my guests. They've missed meeting everyone from a princess to a fire-eater. I hope he's not so careless with matches!

I have vivid memories of being asked to a charity event. The printed invitation was preceded by a phone call to enlist my co-operation. And the day before, another phone call reminded me of the charity's importance. The event was to be held in a street close to my shop in the West End of London. There was no house number on the invitation, but I felt I knew the street well and thought that '... House' would be easy to find – how wrong I was. I drove up and down the street a couple of times. Then I asked at a pub, then I asked at a still-open shop. At each place I asked, the answer was the same: 'We've just had David Steel in here looking for it too.' Other couples joined me in the search. We even got to a telephone and contacted the charity's office, only to find, of course, the answering machine turned on. Bob Monkhouse seems to have been the only guest who managed to find the place, and the party was much depleted.

You should always give people a brief idea of what to expect in the way of catering. If you invite them for seven, do you want them gone by nine or are you expecting them to stay with you for dancing and breakfast? If you don't make it clear, some people will make dinner plans, and others will stay till you come downstairs in your dressing gown! Be a little modest, but try not to be misleading. If you ask people for drinks, they won't expect to stay for dinner! Though I'll never forget the time I, and about half a dozen other friends, was asked to 'spend an evening' at someone's house. On arrival, around half past seven, we were only offered a spot of wine in the bottom of those glasses people used to use for liqueurs, no bigger than thimbles; a small cake was on a platter on the 'coffee table'. One by one we were taken on a guided tour of a house that might have cost a fair amount of money but had been decorated with such an atrocious lack of taste it was hard to imagine. The owner's bed had lights set into the headboard like a leather-lined spaceship!

It was quite obvious we were none of us expected to leave till the evening had grown late, but nonetheless we were never offered any more ('More,' said Alice, 'I can't have more, I haven't had any to start with') wine, nor was the cake ever cut. If our host and hostess felt too weak to do this, they could have asked their au pair, who was right next door in their kitchen. At a social gathering some time later, this man was boasting how he'd got the turnover of his business up to £2 million a month! Turning to me, his wife said, 'You must come round to us for an evening soon!'

With great conversation, warmth and wit you could get away with entertaining for hours on almost just glasses of water (if you were really broke you could always buy a few vegetable/cooking dyes, serve coloured waters and I wonder if anyone would notice if you stuck a

cherry or olive in the glass?). It doesn't take much to make you appear generous with a pot of tea!

I usually ask people to drinks for 6.30–8.30 or 7–9, and although I stop serving wine around 9 or 9.30, I find people stay well past 10, even to 10.30 and beyond. If you can afford it, I think it helps to break the tension most people feel at the beginning of a party to have a few of what they'd call in America 'hors-d'oeuvres': drink alone is not enough. Here people put bits of cheese and pineapple on Ritz crackers. There they're a little more ambitious. My favourite are little rolls of buttered thinly-sliced brown bread with asparagus tips or smoked salmon. It's mad to spend all your money on drink and none on food. If you're on a tight budget, crisps are really a help! Make sure they're fresh and buy lots. Home-made cheese straws are a nuisance to make but they're much appreciated. I have them made using cut out children's toy shapes like butterflies, lions, hearts, flowers, or occasionally initials. We call these Designer Label Cheese Straws! Smarties look jolly, and go down well. Sometimes we have tiny chocolate cakes with Smarties on, sometimes I make stuffed vine leaves. Try a variation of my Ascot recipe.

You've invited your friends to a party. What are you going to do with them? Will you be able to answer the door yourself, greet them, introduce them and pour drinks for them? Will they be wearing coats, and if so where will you put them? Will anyone need to stay the night, and if so do you need to make special preparations for them? What toilet facilities have you set aside for your guests? Some small parties need 'games' to be organized to get them going. Everyone loves Chinese whispers, if you're seated around a room, or there's charades. If it's so long since you've played you've forgotten how, just think of 'Give us a clue'. It's terrible to have to think about it before the party's even begun, but when will you want them to leave – and how will you make sure they do – and now how will you make sure they don't want to before that time comes?

I would say to most of you first be yourself and relax, but having just been to a party in a millionaire's home with a multi-million dollar art collection and been offered a buffet of Chinese take-away (and the rice ran out) – if that's being you, then don't be. Party time is not a time to think small. Luckily, a lot of drinks companies do allow you to return unopened bottles – and they'll hire you wine glasses. You can find stores that lend glasses free, even. So get plenty of drinks in, but don't forget the soft drinks. As for food, think plenty for your money. Crisps, and if the weather's not too cold try giving crudités: that is a good selection of raw vegetables like cauliflower, celery, carrots, cut up into easy-to-manage size pieces, which is generally well received. A good sauce to dip into is great (unless you fear for your carpet). I never serve red wine at parties. It's far too dangerous when it gets spilt, either for your belongings or if it gets spilt over a guest! If you do spill red wine, pour white wine over it straight away and the stain just disappears. It takes courage to do it for the first time but believe me it's always worked for me. (No solicitors' letters, please.)

I once took a girl to a movie premiere; she fancied a friend of mine and I quite honestly was happier talking to *his* girlfriend. Suddenly, accidentally-on-purpose at the star-studded party afterwards, the girl I'd gone with tipped her glass of wine all over the other girl's head, with very little apology. Her hair was ruined, and her dress too, and by the time she'd returned from tidying herself in the toilet, her boyfriend had gone off with her 'assailant' – he married her six months later and they now have several children!

Special parties

Some of the best parties I've been to have been masked. A mask happens to be about the only item in my home that was actually made in my workroom – I've avoided bringing work home to the house. It's in gold lamé, with diamanté around the eyes and is on a long handle, also covered in gold lamé and then trimmed with gold cherry blossoms made from the same material. It's in a corner by the chimney piece.

We often make masks to order for exotic international parties for clients (and for their menfolk). The masks have to be as beautiful as, and to match, their outfits. One of the most beautiful was created from silk rose leaves to match a shaded silk dress in colours toning through all the autumnal colours from bronze to olive green. It appeared in the London *Times*, and now the owner has it framed and it's hung on a study wall. I usually like severe masks, though I once went to a masked party in what *Tatler* described as 'a pearl-encrusted black sequinned helmet with a resplendent red plume'. Perhaps the most lavish masked party I've been to marked the re-opening of the Dorchester Hotel's restaurant, and was in aid of the Royal Opera House. When the pudding arrived, it was preceded by a parade of chefs. Each carried a two-foot-high letter, carved in glistening ice, spelling out 'R-O-Y-A-L O-P-E-R-A H-O-U-S-E'. The masks were quite upstaged.

Fancy dress parties: it's so difficult to know just how far to go. An actress friend, Rikki Howard, who was a chalet maid in 'Hi-De-Hi' asked me to her engagement party, come 'as your favourite film role'. I couldn't decide, since I don't really have secret longings to be Humphrey Bogart or James Dean, so I was stuck, till I decided to go as possibly the most famous roll of film at that time – the Andrex puppy! When I saw her, I found my hostess had gone for blonde bombshell glamour, though I couldn't place her as anyone in particular. Apart from her fiancé – who opened the door as Superman, complete with knickers over his tights – and a few guys with greased-down hair who could have been Fred Astaires or Valentinos, no one else was so dressed up.

Imagine how dubious I felt when I was phoned up to go to another friend's a week later. 'Oh, and by the way, it's fancy dress,' they added in a casual way. He was a really old friend, I thought I really knew, a director of his father's thriving fur business and just married. She was settling down nicely in a fabulous North London mansion. I wasn't going to make the same mistake twice in the same month. I didn't mind dressing up a bit – but *fancy* dress? No, not again.

I rang the doorbell. I could hear the early sounds of a successful party about to begin.

The door opened and there they were – she was a pregnant pumpkin, complete with hat with a twirly stalk and he was dressed as the black butler/maid in *Cage aux Folles*, complete with tutu and suspenders, and there behind them were several Draculas, punks, an eighteenth-century courtier, a couple of Romans, a Greek and a ghost. I had to leave early, I couldn't stand people asking me what on earth I'd come as.

Perth in Australia may seem a long way to go for a fancy dress party, but the man who has come to be known as the Party King of Perth really knows how to throw them! Areas of the town are closed off, so famous have they become. If you're lucky enough to be invited to one, you'll have to come in authentic style – but this is made easier because with your invitation you'll receive instructions on what to wear. In 1985 he gave a party on the theme of *Gone With the Wind*, so women were told the correct sizes of hoops for their crinolines, men the fashionable heights for their hats. He'd even arranged for several dressmakers to be available for those who needed them.

Set in three locations, the party climaxed by a river with the full Tara conflagration; it had begun decorously enough in a hotel, when the 240 guests were startled by a troop of cavalry bearing down on them and announcing the outbreak of the Civil War. Every detail is researched, and for that party 120 extras were employed. The previous year's *Titanic* party ended, of course, with the full catastrophe, sinking and all. Happily, everyone survived – though a few had such terrible hangovers, for a day or two it was touch and go.

It *is* fun to have a fancy dress party, and one way to help your friends to enjoy it as much as you should is to give it a theme you can follow through with the food and drink. Black and gold, or red and gold parties are very festive and easy for your guests. For a black and white party, you could hire an ultra violet light or a strobe. You could ask people to wear spots or stripes and decorate food with smarties and chocolate drops, use black olives and lay food in strips and stripes. Twenties parties are a little corny, as are tarts and vicars parties now. If you give your guests enough warning, you can take them further back in time, just pick your century – and maybe suggest a few paintings they could base their outfits on. Oriental parties, tropical parties or Roman or Greek will be less costly on your guests (though Roman parties generally turn out to be orgies). Don't even consider giving a pyjama party!

Your favourite Hollywood character might be fun, despite what I've said and could end up as quite an inexpensive party if you're a bit broke because instead of serving alcohol you could declare prohibition and give tea in cups (although in prohibition times it was reputedly bath tub gin or whisky) or if drink isn't that important to your friends, call it an evening tea dance.

Or you could have a M*A*S*H party – show videos of M*A*S*H and your guests could come in any style gear, or come as corpses! Here again, food needn't cost a lot; just serve lots of beer and ketchup.

Tiaras and tophats sounds rather a good idea, not to be taken too seriously – hopefully the men will wear white tie and tails! This is what most men wore at the Irish Georgian Society's 1985 Ruritanian Ball, in a beautiful house in Regent's Park, although some men rose to the occasion with colourful uniforms suitably bemedalled and sashed. The women had loads of glittering jewellery, much of it real and a small band played everything but rock. The committee for a fancy dress party to raise money for the Leighton House Museum I was on invited guests to come 'Aesthetic'; and one guest turned up as a peacock. Two weeks later I was round the corner at the Commonwealth Institute at a graduate design show and dinner, hosted by the Secretary of State for

Scotland. The invitation stated black tie or Highland dress; but, being a fashion party, someone turned up dressed as a peacock – a girl, this time.

Embassy parties often look like fancy dress parties if the diplomats wear their native dress, and others come in their uniforms. For instance, the Egyptian Embassy celebrating their National day looked absolutely spendid. Being met by the charming host and hostess under the chandeliered and gilded ceilings of the embassy in South Audley Street, in London's West End, didn't prepare me for the sight of several hundred guests in the gardens in such a range of outfits: ethnic, uniform or simply dressed-up. The scene, if it hadn't been for the waiters darting to and fro with trays laden with drink and delicious canapés, resembled the back lot of a busy and diverse Hollywood film company!

Even if you're not an ambassador, you could always issue invitations with this type of theme, or you could call it Colonial Garden Party, or 'Casablanca'. One of the wildest parties in 1984 was thrown (literally – there was the swimming pool to prove it) by the Thompson Twins at Stocks, Victor Lownes' country estate. Hundreds left the security of London to venture far up the M1, decked out as requested as 'Sleazy Aristocrats'. It was a great party because there was so much to see and do, and rock stars galore. A conservatory with potted palms gave credence to solar energy – the third Thompson Twin, Alana, in black lace, seemed to be everywhere in and out. On the lawns there were inflatables and also cabaret acts. I just put a wide red sash diagonally across a cream silk jacket, and left it to hang at the side with a bow. It was held in place with a diamond brooch that looked like a decoration (but it wasn't – it was a real family heirloom). The 'aristocracy' vied for attention with the hullabaloo, rows of pinball machines, indoor and outdoor swimming pools and eventually and inevitably the jacuzzis. Breakfast was served around two – I left around three, but I believe some guests were there twenty four hours later!

How about having a conjuror at your party? Several young people seem to be interested in presenting magic in new and interesting ways, although none of them have hit the big time yet. A nightclub opening I went to had a conjuror who went round amongst the guests, like Jason Connery and Prince and Princess Stefano Massimo and Lady Edith Foxwell, and performed little tricks of sleight of hand that, although simple, were astonishing because they were performed close to. And at the Reform Club a friend had his guests, mostly MPs and 'captains of industry', entertained by a magician who 'juggled' – which was perhaps even more appropriate! And I'll always remember Ossie Clark's 'Black Magic' fashion show where not only the clothes were magic, but a conjuror came on and did his bit too!

A wedding is the most formal party most people get involved in. Etiquette is involved, however small the guest list, and the guest list always presents problems and there seems to be a million and one other do's and don'ts, many of them outdated. The trouble is these all come at a time when the marrying couple have enough other more real things to worry about. Nowadays more couples are involved in planning their own wedding, and it may even be a second wedding for one or both of them, with even more likelihood of complications.

Wedding presents of course are expected, but nowadays they needn't be practical things – especially if it's a second wedding or the bride or groom have been keeping home for some time before – one may even be moving into the home of the other, or they may have been living together, even for some time! A list chosen at a convenient store by the couple is both helpful to them and to guests who are unsure what they should buy and would rather not waste money on the 'wrong' thing. On the other hand I know that lists are sent out by some people with the wedding invitations but this should be done with a degree of sensitivity. Not everyone wants to receive a list headed – car, fridge-freezer, first-class tickets for two to Barbados! Even if the couple feel they have guests who could afford these luxuries, the act of arranging a list with a large department store could save embarrassing less well off or closely connected guests – and some special guests could be singled out for the really 'special present' list.

The other ordeal of a wedding is speechmaking. A lot of people are terrified of making a speech. An acquaintance told me how terrible a speech he'd made, and yet I'd actually heard him recite it, word perfect, 36 hours before it was needed. In fact I was quite jealous – I have never been able to say my speeches word perfect so far ahead. 'And what's so terrible was, I'm great at improvisation,' he said.

'Why didn't you read it?' I asked naively – I knew then what the problem was; he obviously hadn't kept to his script.

First rule of speech making:
Keep it brief!

Second rule:
Keept it to the point!
(Unless you're terribly, terribly witty;
even if you are, stick to Rule I.)

Third rule:
If you've a script – stick to it.

I often read my speeches word for word. Of course I can 'ad lib' a thank you, or improvise as well if I have to. Radio phone-ins are fun, for instance. Before any live interviews I'm a real bundle of nerves, but once we're on the air there is no time to be nervous. Questions and answers are only an informal form of speechmaking.

Once you've decided to read a set speech, you shouldn't improvise away from it at all – you'll find you're fishing for words to get back, start stuttering and then you're lost.

If you are going to read your speech it shouldn't sound pompous and 'written'. The trick is to write it so it sounds natural. You should write it well in advance, to give you the time to become really familiar with it, so you don't have your head down over the pages of script all the time. I usually write my speeches out in block capitals, so that it's easy to read them. When I gave my talk to the Patrons of the Costume Council of the Los Angeles County Museum, after we'd shown the first set of slides, the lights didn't come on again, and in the dark I had to try to make out the outline of my writing. Luckily, I knew my script well enough to get me to a point where I could stop and ask for the lights to be put on. Hearing a disembodied voice might be the right type of delivery in a Vincent Price movie, but didn't quite suit a lecture on fashion and hats!

Too many people try too hard when they're talking or giving a speech. If you're giving a speech of thanks – do just that. I think up to a few years ago people expected to hear jokes with their speeches but nowadays if you don't want to tell, or aren't good at telling jokes, don't bother. Your audience is probably too sophisticated anyway – or if not and they want jokes let them go home and listen to their favourite tapes or album.

If you're going to ad lib then at least give yourself some cue-cards – write a short list of headings, and beware – time always goes faster than you think. People being interviewed on television for the first few times don't realize how quickly time flies. When they're told they've had three or four minutes air time they can't believe it – and a three or four minute interview usually seems plenty long enough when you're the viewer!

The German Embassy in London have a way of making you talk. Arriving for a grand formal dinner with the Sinden family, I was looking forward to being with them. We were asked to pick numbers from two baskets, one holding pink 'lottery' type tickets, the other blue. I thought it was very generous to give prizes simply for turning up! Attending parties at Embassies you never know what might happen – I was less delighted when told that actually we'd just chosen our table numbers, and that was their idea for getting everyone to relax and mix! I conquered my first thoughts of terror, but remained uneasy throughout what proved a delicious meal, and in charming company – although the lady to my left didn't speak a word of English, she had a nice smile and I hope mine was 'Colgate' fresh too! Everyone else I spoke to after that evening felt 'thrown in at the deep end' and I wouldn't suggest trying it on guests, unless you have to have a family gathering where there is no other way out!

Dogs are about to take parties over! It started a couple of years ago. Elaine Paige arrived at one of my parties with a straw basket beribboned, and her tiny puppy (Terrier Tugger) inside! The puppy wasn't big enough for a ribbon. And then Lady Settrington arrived with her huge but beautifully behaved Irish Wolfhound, Folly. Diana Cooper never arrived at a party without her Chihuahua, Doggie.

Nowadays I don't expect to go to a private party (and they're the smartest) where there aren't canine guests! Lady Henrietta Rous's Christmas party list included Ossie Clark's dog, Oscar, who is a cousin to her own Ziggie. Zephyr, who is Nicky Haslam's adorable black long-haired Peke, is even on the committee of a charity ball, and once dogs get on these there would seem to be no end to it. And of course they attract all the love and attention. My 'doggie' an adorable white Alsatian, is the only creature I know to get away with visiting a famous Bond Street fashion store and not buying anything! And still not get treated like a dog. So my advice to you is, if you've got a dog, flaunt it. Mind you the same does *not* go for children. Dogs may go where children shouldn't tread. Perhaps because most of these 'social' canines are better behaved than most children would be.

The smartest dog of all I bumped into at a party recently is Professor Pom-Pom, a Standard Poodle. His fame is entirely due to his own cleverness, not that of his owner. He goes daily to London University to accompany his mistress to work. When a chair became vacant, he was put forward as the best candidate and has become the temporary occupant.

Bad conversation is 'How are you doing?'. '*Who* are you doing?' is much more interesting. 'What are you doing?' is perhaps worst of all, so much hangs on your answer. It's much politer to ask nowadays if you are working than what do you do, but the worst case of snobbery came when an Australian asked me this question, some years ago. I was at a party of Homi Masandi, called the Caviar Queen of London because of the huge amounts of it at her legendary parties. There was David Frost, the Shah of Iran's sister, Georgie Fame to play piano... Seated next to me at dinner was Kerry Packer, the Australian television magnate who eventually, after eyeing the cleavage of my pretty blonde guest between us, asked the inevitable 'what do you do' and I, perhaps on reflection naively, said 'I make hats'. 'Hats,' he repeated to himself, pausing long enough only to turn to my right to Sir Charles Clore. 'And what do you do?' he asked. 'I make shoes,' answered Sir Charles, who failed to add that in fact this meant he owned more shoe shops than anyone else, and Selfridges too! Kerry Packer returned to my female companion for the rest of the meal, and didn't speak one word more to the two of us. I had always thought this the end of the story, but then at a birthday party given at the Harley Street home of Lady (Jackie) Killearn for her own birthday, Homi recounted to guests who included the Duchess of Argyll, the sequel. She had had a telephone call following the party from Sir James Goldsmith, quite bewildered, who said Kerry Packer had phoned him saying how eccentric her party was because he had been at dinner on a table with her hat-maker and her shoe-maker!

I can only hope that Sir Charles Clore was rewarded for his generosity to me when he got to the pearly gates by St Peter saying 'Oh! A shoe-maker. Well, you must meet my friend – he walks on water.'

Party pointers

Entertain generously – whether it is two or two hundred.

Don't ever use paper cups.

Use candles, but don't stick them in children's jelly mould cases.

Plastic forks are disgusting.

Disconnect the phone for the night – this is not your meanness, it presupposes (flatteringly) that your guests are going to be phoning Hong Kong, New York etc.

Champagne can be good value. People respect it.

Mix wine with tonic/lemonade or whatever to make an economical punch.

Never give red wine if you love your carpets/furniture.

Give the party a theme – fancy dress, an overall colour, a special event, someone's birthday or anniversary.

Give a night-time tea-dance if you're really broke.

And beware of taking parties and party-going too seriously. One Thursday I went to a party, left quite early and had gone to bed when the phone rang.

'I hear you were at a party,' said a friend who hadn't been invited. 'X saw you there. He said you looked so awfully tired and ill you must go away on holiday immediately.' I went into a decline straight away, which didn't help me sleep.

I had a nine o'clock appointment the next morning to attend a fitting at the Emanuels, and I felt even worse by then. I told them about this phone call, and David said, 'Thank goodness your enemies don't call you late at night.' I started to feel much better after that bit of Welsh logic!

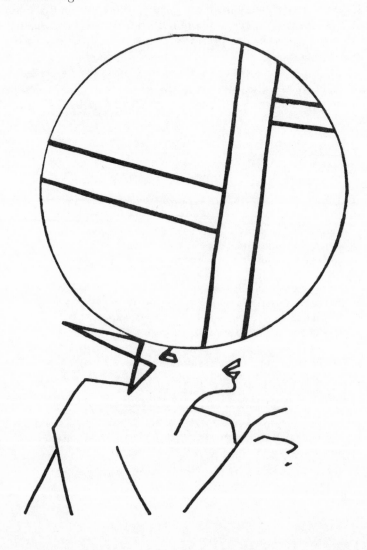

Beauty

$\mathcal{P}$icture one of my shows at Claridges. The room is grandly stuccoed with high ceilings, and chandeliers twinkle. Gilt chairs are arranged around the room and small bay trees at one end indicate where the models will emerge. But most glittering of all, you notice three of the greatest British beauties of our age together for this big occasion. It was thrilling to see Lady Diana Cooper, Marie Helvin and the Duchess of Argyll facing each other not on but across the catwalk, not only because of the obvious ever-present 'beauty' but because there was no magic formula that was common to all of them except perhaps an inner warmth, a glow, a sparkle, from somewhere inside. It was a great opportunity for me to study beauty. What was it in particular that made them beautiful? The shape of nose, mouth, cheekbones? Even when the models came on, like Annabel Heseltine and Joanna Percy, what magic formula could I learn from them? Where was the secret, and could I capture it and bottle it? Before I go any further let me tell you now I am not going to fall in the trap of many other books. I can't promise you instant beauty if you follow my formula. Every beauty reaches that goal their own individual way. With some it's a hard job, a daily grind, for others it comes more naturally. But no one else can do it for you. The only person who can make you beautiful is *you*! But what I am absolutely convinced about is that each and every one, yes you, you and you, can be beautiful as long as you really want to be.

A lot of people will probably think, of course, anyone can be beautiful; give them designer clothes, fabulous furs, jewels, send them to a great hairdresser. But you've seen these type of articles in magazines that attempt a transformation, and I'm the first to admit it just doesn't work like that. I am saying you don't need to spend a vast amount of money to be more beautiful than you are now. Start with some of the basics – many of them are free! For instance, sleep. Few people look their best when they haven't had enough sleep. Now I love staying up at night... partying and having a good time, and I'm sure having a dull life has never been a successful formula for becoming beautiful. In fact, falling in love is often one of the greatest ways to make a person sparkle and that's never dull!

If you have late nights and early mornings, either for work or family reasons, make use of your weekends to get the rest you need or have a regular day off. Take your time off seriously because you won't function properly if you don't. It's a long term regime of rest and play that you need to plan, and on those days when you feel you're looking rotten, just try to get more relaxed. It's one of the advantages of living on your own

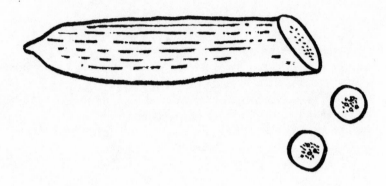

that you can grab an early night whenever you want. A couple of extra hours' sleep uninterrupted by children and cooking meals. No one can really tell you how to relax. In fact, it's a bit like telling someone to be funny, which makes it quite impossible. You probably do know how, but don't think about the triggers: is it a favourite chair, a quick bath, a certain something to put in the bath, listening to a certain piece of music or a tape of favourite sounds (the sea, a beautiful summer's day in the country...)? You don't have to buy these – make your own. While you're relaxing, nothing beats slices of cucumber on the eyes for freshening up.

When I was first asked to do TV interviews, I always used to be very uncomfortable; the heat from the studio lights really felt as if it was burning me. And although the actual screen time of an interview was only a couple of minutes, the length of time I was under the lights was very much more. This burning on the skin and the brightness of the lights made me appear uncomfortable in front of the cameras. And the more I was aware of it, the more uncomfortable I was... But when I next did a TV show I had just come back from abroad. I went in front of the lights and suddenly I realized I'd just paid a fortune to fry under the sun! If I shut my eyes and pretended it was sunshine, my whole attitude to television could change. Now when I go into a studio I think 'beach', and let the cameras do their work.

I infinitely prefer doing radio, where you wander into the studio, sit down and away you go, no lighting rehearsals, camera positions, the paraphernalia of television. But best of all – you don't have to look your best! Nobody'll ever know. Once I arrived at the BBC to do a very early morning show wearing my pyjamas under a floor length mink coat, and the interviewer never even mentioned it. But it's more than that even. When I'm interviewed about fashion and design, I know people are going to criticize how I look, in a way they don't judge politicians, say. (Personally, I think it is disgraceful how most of *them* do look - you wouldn't find me buying a used motor vehicle from one, and that's even before he opened his mouth.) But when you're in the fashion business it's quite difficult to maintain your interest in how you look day after day, especially when you know how long it takes to make the perfect image, the photograph of a model in a newspaper or magazine.

Professional shoppers, known as stylists, get together the wardrobes for TV and advertising. A friend, who is a director of a TV production company, wanted a high-fashion look for an ad he was making. He wasn't satisfied with the clothes bought in by the stylist at around five o'clock; they were due to shoot the next day. So, rather than hold things up, while the stylist went round again in the morning, he went straight off to Harvey Nichols and arrived just as the store was closing. It stayed open an hour for him and he spent around £500 - not a lot, in my opinion, for the service he received!

After the stylist has found enough clothes and accessories to achieve the 'look' they're after (and quality of finish and lastability is almost never the object; what matters is that things photograph well) the fashion editor and one or two assistants choose what they want to take with them on the 'shoot'. They might even choose an exotic location abroad. They've also chosen not only the model, but the photographer, who's got an assistant, the make-up artist and the hairdresser, who's probably got a helper too. And add to this all the photographic equipment, backdrops, lighting, and a few pins and tucks you don't see in the frock, and as long as you start at nine and allow two to three hours make-up time, and several rolls of film, you achieve your 'model' picture. No wonder most fashion editors, with only a few exceptions, look so dreadful. They give up!

So don't feel frustrated if you don't look like the girls or guys in the fashion magazines every day - they don't either. Well only for one flash. But that doesn't mean you shouldn't try to look your best. It is extraordinary that local councils have such strict control over the look of buildings that get put up, and there is always public outrage at the proposal to erect any new building - but no one has the power to fine or imprison someone who looks unnecessarily unattractive. There's a scandalous injustice there somewhere! It's often said of British women that they only have time for their gardens and their dogs - I think that's less true now than it was, but there's still a lot of room for improvement.

When I was doing a regular series on Radio London on fashion I always got letters from women complaining they couldn't find fashionable-looking clothes in sizes over 16. But if you're over size 16 and unhappy, you should probably lose some weight. I sympathize that for medical reasons some people unavoidably are fat. It's possible to be large and glamorous but to all those who say there is no such thing as 'a look' in fashion today I always have to admit that there is.

Models' beauty tips

Use an old mascara brush to brush your eyebrows.

Wash your hair in cold water, never very hot. If you can't stand this, at least make your final rinse cool.

For a professional finish to your make-up, always use a lipbrush. This enables you to get a full-mouthed glamorous look with the lipstick painted into the grain of the lips. Models I know squash their little bits of lipstick into boxes like children's paintboxes, and then mix their own colours with their lipbrush. The best place to buy the boxes is Japan.

Blusher should always be put on last, so that the colour is balanced with your eye make-up and lipstick.

When trying on clothes if you're made up, avoid smudging make-up by putting an old scarf right over your head. Silk chiffon is ideal; see-through, light, won't disturb your hair, and it doesn't slip.

Go carefully with eye shadow – matching shadow to your outfit is as ageing as a blue rinse. Choose colours to co-ordinate with your clothes, or choose a shade to highlight a complementary fashion colour.

If you want your skin to look good, try drinking a glass of hot water with a slice of lemon before anything else in the morning. I know several models who start each day this way.

Looking good makes you feel good. When you *feel* good you'll look good. The two things complement each other. You can wear your skirts short or long, your hair curled or straight, men can wear suits or casuals, you can be tall, short, blond(e) or dark, there are no particular apparent standards of beauty, you can make the best of a bad nose, you don't need to have it 'done', but there is one underlying factor to looking good – you have to have shape. It's not even as easy as it was in the Twiggy era, when all you had to do was look anorexic – and so you could just stop eating to be good-looking. Now you have to be slim, but give an appearance of body – that is, shape. Your waist should be in the right place even if your heart isn't!

Most people are told that you can only be a good shape if you do exercises regularly, and they give up. At school I hated doing exercises and I can't go back into a gym without feeling pangs of remorse. I'd rather not be reminded that boxing was compulsory in my school for a short while – but why did I have to bash up my classmates according to the rules for an hour a week!

I detest all forms of violence, but that doesn't mean I can't defend myself. When I was about 13, I went privately to Mickey Wood's gym in Paddington Street (it's now Pineapple West!) with a couple of friends from school to learn self defence. The oldest of us arranged the terms (I can't remember what they were) and we soon learnt pressure points; how, in real life, people come towards you holding a gun close in to the hip and not at arm's length (they do that in the movies to look glamorous) how the weakest points of the body are vulnerable whether you're small or a giant. Another reason we chose Mickey Wood's gym was because he had taught Sophia Loren to throw Peter Sellers into the Thames in the film *The Millionairess* and her photo was on display outside! On several occasions it was rumoured that the Krays were coming after our private lessons were over, and once or twice we lingered in the changing rooms to glimpse the next arrivals – not really knowing the difference between the Krays and the other 'stars' who might have attended the gym.

So now all I do is have an active life – hope and am diet-conscious.

If I just want to lose a bit of weight and put myself back on course again, I might do a two-day diet just having a drink of squeezed orange, lemon, mashed banana and a teaspoon of honey, freshly made and drunk three times a day. I used to follow a more drastic eight-day diet, though now I try to be more sensible. While I acknowledge it can't do your body much good, a Harley Street dietician told me to go ahead and do it if I'd be unhappy otherwise. All it needs is discipline; try it one day at a time – and it's much less nasty than it sounds. For two days at a time eat only fresh apples; then decide on either chicken or fish; cheeses; finally citrus fruit. Drink only water or black coffee. Suddenly you start to appreciate the difference in taste and texture between green and red apples, Cheddar and Cheshire, oranges and grapefruit as never before. By the time you've finished the eight days, not only will you be thinner, you will eat less for several days and appreciate the taste of your food more.

I thought I'd shock Audrey Eyton (whose book *The F-Plan Diet* sold two million in this country alone – I should think you've got one in the house somewhere) when I told her about these diets, but she said that all cutting down of calorie intake is good for you – although on that particular evening she had ordered blackcurrant fool and 'had a taste' of my bananas in custard with rum. And the last time I saw Judy Mazel, who wrote *The Beverly Hills Diet Book*, was in Ma Maison – and she was eating more than pineapple. That should cheer us all up.

I do try and watch my diet. (This doesn't mean I don't eat crisps and chocolates too!) As a general rule I stick to fresh foods and eat in moderation. If you eat light you feel light, and you don't mind walking rather than taking the bus or going up flights of stairs instead of taking the lift! If you've lovely enticing cream cakes in the fridge, *of course* you're going to eat them. It's a pity for them to go to waste, so think before you buy them. If you share your life with someone who's a bit of a fatty, do some thinking on their behalf. They'd probably be a bit happier if they were a bit slimmer, so either stock the larder a little less selfishly, or buy appetising fresh food, pears and grapes, apples, salad stuffs, sticks of celery – and put a sign on the fridge door that's a reminder to watch your figure, if you want people to watch your body!

Now we've disposed of dieting, I'll confess that I'm not a great one for exercise, either. Luckily I live in a five-storey house so I get exercise in the morning by going downstairs to see if the post's come! But if you don't feel fit, it's easy enough to get more exercise into your life. Walk a little bit extra when the weather's nice. If you smoke walk to the shops to get your cigarettes! If you fancy working out with light weights, you don't have to rush out and buy them. Use bags of sugar; even cans of beans will do.

I walk to and from work, but then I'm well placed to do so, it's a nice seven or eight minutes each way. I should swim really – there's a swimming pool at the end of the road. I don't go often: it's not just the hassle of getting dressed to go there, and getting dressed after the swim, and drying the hair. The trouble is that there's always a crowd of people in the pool. The first time I went I swam lengths and all these people who were swimming widths kept bumping into me. I had a terrible time! I'm not going to be put off, I thought, I need this exercise. I'll go back and swim widths. When I did, everyone was doing lengths. You can't even swim underwater there, with people diving in all over the place!

I find ski-ing and water ski-ing too much like hard work. Apre's ski is quite enough exercise for me and certainly exhausting enough! (You can't beat the Palace Hotel, St Moritz for this.) Helicopter ski-ing sounds sensible, although I haven't done it myself. My friend Lucy Williams, tells me you hire a helicopter for the day and this whisks you off to the slopes where you don't normally run and sets you down far from the madding crowd, possibly with a guide if you go to a really 'unknown' area. Then you don't have to share your slopes but, and best of all, you avoid all the dreadful queues for the ski-lifts!

I was once asked to design a glamorous ski-cap for the 'Ski-Show'. I made it in black velvet, with the white piste in white arctic fox, complete with a gold-clad skier and a couple of small model pine trees any builder of model railways would be proud of. I was then quoted in the *Daily Mail* as saying that the reason I don't go ski-ing is that I can't stand the hideous ski-caps!

Tips for would-be skiers must be (a) don't wear a bobble on your cap, (b) don't wear your socks outside your trousers, (c) remember it's *Gluhwein* in German, but *vin chaud* in French!

What's finally put me off ski-ing is not the accidents I might do to myself, but the fear of the damage done to quite innocent people by those hurling themselves round willy-nilly – especially after lunch!

Water ski-ing I hate because it's simply too much effort on the arms if you're not a regular, and you have to have a good person you trust in the boat. I do enjoy jet-ski-ing. If you've not seen it, I should explain that you ride a machine a bit like a little motorbike and it whizzes over the water like a mini motor boat. My first experience with one was a strange début! It was at Calvi in Corsica, where there wasn't much else to amuse me. I got up on the ski – it's not much different to standing up on a motorbike, except that you're riding on water. Once you've got up there, you feel terrific. I was riding parallel to the shore, feeling terrific – and of course that's when I slipped off. The jet-ski has an automatic cut-out, so it's not dangerous and doesn't go too far away – but as I fell the huge wash created by the machine managed, with the fall, to fill my swimming trunks with water. They instantly fell off, to the wild and appreciative applause from the watching crowd on the shore! There's no better game than a show-off de-bagged!

The film *Pumping Iron II: The Women*, immediately gave me the feeling here was a new look for women that would have an effect on the 'Ideal' we have of the way they look, even if it takes ten years to catch on. Just as when I saw Arnold Schwartzenegger in *Pumping Iron* I felt that many men would become interested in body-building, even though when it first came out most were sniggering at it. (The essence of

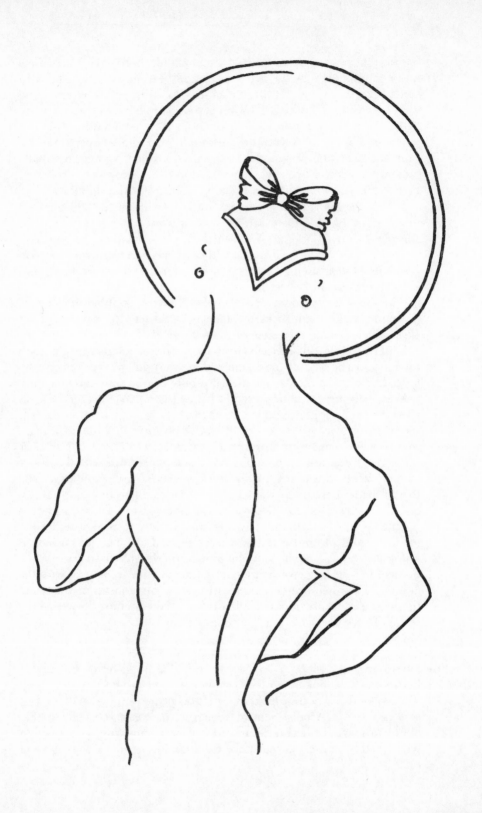

fashion is timing. A fashion is first laughed at because it shocks, then it establishes itself, and finally it is laughed at again when it becomes outmoded. Platform shoes are a great example of this. We all laugh at them now, even if we were quite happy to stagger around on top of them only a decade ago.)

The years have passed and Schwartzenegger is now rich and famous, not at all to be laughed at, and the developed physique is more than just accepted for men - it is positively the desired look for a large part of the fashion industry.

The following night, at a dinner party, I told the actress next to me how I loved *Pumping Iron II*, and was surprised when she told me she did Nautilus training and offered me her biceps - and she was not a freak. She was Lady Marsha Fitzalan Howard, daughter of the Duke of Norfolk, married to actor Patrick Ryecart - and mother of two daughters. Even more to the point, four out of five of the girls then started to preen and pose, owning up that they were doing some sort of training whereas the men, who consisted of both theatre and business people, couldn't muster more than an occasional jogger and someone who used to play squash. I like shapely women - yes I know I'm a chauvinist - but it may be good news that shapely nowadays doesn't just mean a big pair of you-know-whats! More her pectorals too! And it's much more fair - any woman who wants to can build her own body.

Of course I wanted to show my hats off on the new 'shape' woman. The best way I know to show hats is with the models wearing nothing but leotards, tights, high heeled shoes and over-the-elbow gloves. I was lucky when a friend discovered Caroline Cheshire, the body builder, pretty and blonde, definitely attractive. Following nine other models down the catwalk in the ballroom of the Grosvenor House Hotel, she raised a few eyebrows. Although at first glance she looked no more athletically built than some of the other girls, she stunned the audience as she did a few poses to show off her physique.

It so happens she didn't wear a veiled pillbox - but she could have done!

Having your hair done

You should leave cutting your hair to an expert. Don't grab the scissors in a moment of boredom and hack the back; you'll regret it, even if it does save you a few pounds. And don't rush off to a hairdresser and ask him to cut all your hair off because you hope it'll change your life. That only happened to Thoroughly Modern Millie because she wanted it to happen, and there was that wicked Chinese washerwoman. If you notice one lurking, then do get your hair bobbed – but under any other circumstances it won't make as much difference as you think. (It's the same with nose jobs. A friend who's now Beauty Editor of one of the glossiest fashion mags admitted she'd thought that when she had her nose altered it would change her entirely. It didn't, she just got a new nose; not a new life, but a new slant on it.)

One cosmetics PR I know goes to the hairdresser every morning, and many people do go regularly several times a week. The rich have their hairdressers go to them. But for most people, a visit to the hairdresser is only made when they want a cut, or a new look. So make sure your hairdresser knows you want a style that's easy enough for you to manage on your own.

Hair can be the most ageing aspect of a man or woman's appearance. Every now and then, take a hard look at your style and think about changing it to be more in keeping with the latest look. I know one woman who seems to intend going through life with just one hairstyle from her teenage years. She wouldn't dream of going through life with just one partner. In fact, she's had five husbands – but she's still got the beehive hairdo!

When you feel like a change, discuss it with your regular stylist, if you have one, and if you think he or she will understand what you want. If you're choosing a new salon, try to choose one whose work you admire. Take the time to gawp as you pass by – it's easy to see into many salons. They may be surprised, but common sense is on your side: you need to have an idea of what they'll do to you.

If your visits to the hairdresser are very infrequent, go for the best you can afford. If you've seen a picture in a magazine that's wonderful, phone the salon who did it and ask how much they'll charge to cut your hair (beware of extras like expensive conditioners), and ask if VAT and service are included. When you are offered tea or coffee (or champagne at many West End salons) you'll be expected to pay for it – is it worth it to you? (Don't try taking a picnic here, please.) Do make sure your chosen look will suit you; ask them first. Will it need a new wardrobe to complement it. Your hair may be thicker or thinner than the model's. And it may be hard to get an appointment with that stylist, not only because he's good but because magazines tend to like to work with the same people all the time. Top hairdressers are prepared to count the cost of the business they lose while the stylist is doing something for a magazine feature against the expectation of business received as a result of it.

When you're actually at the hairdresser's, if there's any doubt in your mind then don't have your hair cut. Tell them you'd rather wait for another day. If they need the money so badly they get upset, you can be certain they're not terribly good. But if you feel you've taken up a lot of their time, why not ask them just to wash and blowdry your hair. This could give you confidence, it won't cost as much as a cut, and it's a great deal cheaper than a cut you hate. If you are unlucky enough to get one of these, don't rush off and have it cut again – let it grow a bit. In the meantime, you can always wear a hat!

Stylists aren't necessarily colourists. You might be better advised to go to a colouring expert at a different salon if you want a drastic change. If you just want to change your colour for the sake of change, there are some very simple colourings that wash out easily. Of course, it's not just women who want to change the colour of their hair. Men dye their hair, and I don't just mean getting out the Grecian 2000 (what does that phrase mean, by the way?) Just as earrings nowadays don't mean a man's effeminate, neither does hair colouring. But even I was shocked to see that the middle-aged ordinary-looking ticket collector on a train to Ascot wore a single diamond stud – perhaps specially for Royal Ascot week, perhaps because it was his only one. In the Beatles' day, everyone seemed to be dark – now there are Paul Nicholas, Jason Connery, David Gower. Some of the blonds must be getting a little help from their bottle (and I don't just mean drinking more milk).

If you're rich enough, you can ask your hairdresser to put your hat on for you. A top stylist will be delighted to do this, or to set your hair with your tiara. Taking a tiara to the hairdresser's always creates a buzz. Everyone likes to see your jewellery – but be careful not to entrust your diamonds to someone you don't know, or let them out of your sight for long. The worst cautionary tale I know about having your hair done, however, concerns not a tiara but a hat.

A woman went to a salon in London's West End to have her hair done; she wanted it fussed about around her wide-brimmed hat. The salon was on the second floor and when her hair had been preened and teased for over an hour she finished her coffee and bade farewell to her friends – many of whom she was about to see at the racecourse later that day. But no matter which way she turned her head, she could not get down the very narrow staircase.

If you decide to have your hat put on by your hairdresser – certainly a good idea if it's a small hat where the back of the hair shows importantly – make sure you can get out with it on. Remember, too, you may have to get in and out of a car – and maybe even the loo!

Finally, if all else seems to have failed, simply keep telling yourself you're beautiful. I've come in contact with the most beautiful women in the world, and there are odd moments when even they aren't their usual selves. But now that rich women can have everything lifted, from the bottom up (and have the fat literally sucked out), it's good to remember that real beauty comes from within. You shouldn't, however, use this as an excuse to disguise yours too deeply.

Clothes

*I*f money's no object, how about going for the best in the world? That's unquestionably Paris couture, and those workrooms are busier now than they have been for a long time. Although a suit at Dior starts around £5,000, plus around £1,500 for the blouse, and an extravagant evening dress might cost well over £20,000, an embroidered version as much as £30,000, a lot of women think they're worth every penny, cent or centime.

However, even at Dior they no longer have live models for their clients in the salon but rely, like so much of the fashion industry, on having comprehensive videos of their collections, taken at their press showings. These can be played at any time – and of course stopped and re-wound for a client to make her choices!

I too use video: this year filmed with two cameras to get the hats from every angle (top and sides included), and we can show two versions: all the full-length, which lasts around 50 minutes, a three-minute version for the very busy.

When you have a couture dress made, what do you get? You obviously get something that is unique to you, a perfect fit for your figure and made by masters of their art, crafted rather than manufactured. At your fittings you will first try on a toile (a copy of your dress in rough cotton, which will give an idea of the dress on you and it will be used eventually to cut your dress). It is from the toile that skirt length will be judged; you may be given a choice of sleeve, one shoulder may be more exaggerated than the other, the length of sleeve can be determined.

Because of the cost, and also the fine quality of the luxury fabrics used, most of the major work of structure is done on the toile. At Christian Dior, three fittings for an outfit are the minimum. But of course, once a couture house has your measurements, you will not have to visit them so often; they will make up a dummy with your measurements and may do the fittings on that.

If clothes are worth taking that much care over in this life, then what about in the next? I only bother about the quality of life, and never mind about the length, but my family has quite a record of longevity. Ages were seldom discussed, so when I was 19 it came as quite a surprise at my maternal grandmother's birthday dinner at the Savoy (candles flickering, chandeliers glowing, diamond jewellery ablaze) when an uncle said, 'This must be her 98th birthday.' Being an only child, I'd always been close to her, but it had never occurred to me how enormous the age gap was. (It wasn't till years later that I realized the grandfather I'd never known, and so had thought of as dying romantically young, had been over 80 when he passed on.) Both my father's parents reached their nineties; his father was a strong personality even at 92, and managed to cause more people to row than any other person I know. The complexity of his will and the winding up of his affairs are still encouraging an intermittent fracas. I think of him up there, not chuckling (I don't think he could ever have been a very happy man) but smiling – and I laugh too!

The trouble with the afterlife is that though there may be lots of talk about it, it's never from the fashion designer's point of view. None of us know what we'll look like on the other side, but for people who devote their lives to covering their bodies fashionably, or modestly, or at all, the reality of what we'll look like to each other must be significant.

I'd have imagined Paradise to offer a profusion of colours, but there's a widely-held theatrical designers' view that we'll be condemned to wear one outfit – an eternally white shapeless robe seems very boring. What upsets me more is the thought that we might spend eternity in the last clothes we wore on earth. It's bad enough having to decide what one's going to wear of a morning, very off-putting to think that if one's run over that's what one'll be wearing for ever. And how muddled it will look, with people wandering around in the styles of so many millennia. Can you imagine bumping into a neighbour in eight hundred years' time and hearing her say, 'I wish I'd worn my green cashmere!'

Perhaps, on the other hand, you're allowed to choose what you want, in one of those intermediary stages one's heard so much about on the way to the pearly gates. You get to rung 152 on the ladder and there it is, the biggest shop you've ever seen. 'Out of this world,' you hear a woman whistle – even though she's from Dallas, and thought nothing could beat Nieman Marcus. I bet you'd see a line of English people queuing sedately – and everyone else treating it like the china department of Harrods on the first day of the sale.

Or maybe, after all, we won't have clothes; we'll just be immortal souls floating around. This is really frightening. I've no idea what an immortal soul would look like. Are there such things as Page 3 immortal souls? And how would you recognize an immortal soul you know. You could pass by your closest friend, or – even worse – miss a real star like Cleopatra, Tarquin the Proud or Jack the Ripper. It'd be such fun to find King Alfred and then introduce him to Mrs Beeton – difficult enough to spot them wearing their own clothes (though you'd have plenty of time to do it in), but impossible if you had just the immortal soul to go by.

That's one of the advantages of being a hat designer, I suppose. Hats have been going for an awfully long time, so if I met Tutankhamun or Boudicca they'd understand what I'd done for a living – not so if I'd been a computer programmer or a hamburger tycoon.

Back to the serious business. If you haven't got unlimited money for your wardrobe, what follows, I promise you, will help you to feel richer, look even better, and perhaps more effortlessly too. You might even save money – it's certainly not all spend, spend, spend!

I don't think it's necessarily true that if you've a huge amount to spend on your clothes you'll look wonderful. The same time/money principle applies here as in interior decoration. If you're rich, you have someone else to do your pressing for you. If you're not, you either do your own – or choose clothes that don't need pressing! Rich people tend to wear lots of white, especially in the summer – you could build up a summer wardrobe of nothing else – but think of the dry-cleaning bills first.

What do you do to look good? Well, first of all work out how much you've got to spend – do a bit of budgeting, not just when you need a new coat or to cover a party outfit. Make a plan of how much you can realistically spend on clothes during the year. Even if you're rich it's a good idea. Are you going to buy a new fur this year? A new piece of jewellery? A crocodile handbag? Any one of these will last for years, but will require a large initial investment.

Before you go out and spend any money, look at your wardrobe and work out what you've got there already. Clothing has become less seasonal now that people travel more, and central heating and air conditioning all make clothes work longer through the year for us. But some are still summer clothes, and some are winter.

At the start of each season I go through my wardrobe, weeding out things that are unwearable either because they are unseasonal or because I've gone off them. I then banish them, to a cupboard at the top of the house. (You could just pack them in a suitcase under the bed if space is tight.) They're just clutter in the wardrobe, and they are in the way when you are trying to sort out an outfit and want to dress in a hurry. I look through everything: suits, jackets, trousers, shirts, ties, shoes, accessories. When I take the clothes up, I look through what is there already to see if there's anything that merits coming down.

I hate to throw clothes away – I'd rather give them away to a good home. This doesn't always mean giving to a friend. You probably think most of your friends would be insulted if you offered them your old clothes – I'm sure they would if they were worn out, but many of my friends enjoy the clothes I'm tired of because they're new to them. And sometimes Valerie Mendes of the Victoria and Albert Museum comes round and sorts out a few things. A particularly extraordinary pair of platform shoes in patchwork metallic snakeskin are on show in the costume department at the moment! I'm slightly worried that they might be just what I'll be looking for in a few years time; I find that if something's well designed and well made, I can recycle it years later. This does remind one to keep in shape, or is encouraging if you're actually in better shape now than three years ago.

Summer clothing should always be comfortable, the hotter the climate the looser the waistband. In really hot climates, always go for really loose comfortable shapes – forget jean-style slacks and go for baggies. If necessary, invest in a pair of white pure cotton slacks with an extra couple of inches at the waist. Buy pure fabrics, cotton especially; it needn't be expensive if you're budget-conscious. Silk feels beautiful against the skin but it marks with perspiration. Buy T-shirts several sizes too big (at least one with long sleeves, useful for visiting religious shrines, and if you get over-sunburnt). A simple white cotton vest or T-shirt shouldn't cost more than a couple of pounds and you can usually add the summer's latest gimmick, like bits of applied denim and lace, rhinestone beads or make interesting cut-outs with a pair of scissors used boldly. You can also save money by cutting down your old flared trousers into shorts. Leave a bit of length to roll up in a trendy 'Out of Africa' way. For very hot climates remember jackets with side vents really are cooler – vents *do* ventilate.

Even the most hat-hating person should think of buying at least one. If you want to travel with a summer straw, there's no need to put it in a hat box. Simply attach a pair of safety pins to the inside headband and use them to hold a string to carry the hat by when you don't want to wear it. When you do want to you simply slip the string in your pocket or hand luggage.

If you can't afford or can't find a suitable coat for the winter, invest in vests. They needn't be nasty. Choose attractive ones. You can get pure silk vests for skiers that feel great, and keep you deliciously warm whilst they are also light. I wear these, though they're hard to get in London, and also simple cheap, plain white cotton short-sleeved, T-shirts. I buy several so there's always a clean one handy to put on; if I run out, I use an old summer T-shirt instead. (If you don't need the extra insulation, can't afford silk underwear but want to feel sexy, why wear any at all?)

If you've got the space, you don't need to throw anything away each season unless it's worn out. It's worth taking the chance that not wearing something for a year or two will give it new life.

Once you've got all your wardrobe for, say, summer – or winter – assembled, start putting outfits together. Which shoes with which trousers, which coat, scarf, belt, suit, tie, shirt (or dress, skirt, bag, blouse, tights – even make-up colours...). Write these combinations down: it's useful to categorize your outfits and you can use your list to remind yourself of the variety of options you have. Headings could be: Work, Weekend, Informal party, Party, Special occasion, Holidays, Sports. If you've never done this before, I'm pretty sure you'll be surprised at the variety you come up with. I'm even more certain that you'll find it worth all the time you spend.

Unless you're already terribly well organized, this will show you the gaps in your wardrobe for the next six months, and with an idea of what you can afford to spend you can plan what you need to purchase.

Of course, if you're very rich you needn't keep any clothes from season to season – just get them all packed up and sent to a charity shop. I heard of one woman who was so rich she never bothered to return home from holiday with her suitcase. She thought it was easier to give everything away to those less fortunate than herself, and to travel light. If you're more 'careful' (that's polite for mean!) you can send any old clothes in good condition to a 'Nearly New' shop. Unfortunately, you don't get much for men's secondhand clothing – when I once did take two suitcases full to a specialist in Camden Town, I wouldn't have had much over to pay a parking fine if I'd got one. Be warned!

Even if you're terribly rich it's still worth making a list of what sort of outfits you need for the season – and it's never too early to start! After all, directly after the sales the new season's merchandise is in the shops – and even in the sales you are likely to find clothes that are good for the next few months... But I don't think sales are the places for bargains they're made out to be: if something didn't sell at £X it wasn't worth it to people who saw it then, just because it is £½X now is no real reason to buy it. The sales are dangerous, if you don't remember this. They're also dangerous if you buy something wonderful you don't need because it's reduced and then have to buy full-priced accessories to go with it.

When you've got your plan of what you need to buy, and your budget to cover those purchases, be flexible about what you pay for each item.

You might be wise to pay more for a belt than a shirt, or more for a shirt than for a pair of trousers. Just make sure that you're getting enough things for your total outlay. Personally I still feel you get best value in Britain by buying the very cheap or absolutely the best. There are exceptions – world-renowned chain stores doing low-to-middle-priced clothes made to exacting standards – but on the whole you can't do better than invest in a few items that are the very best you can afford. Beautifully cut and made clothes always look good. But beware of fabrics that don't wear well – very fine silks need great care, and pure cashmere is so soft that you can't expect a garment made from it to go on for ever. Silk suits won't wear as well as wool.

However, for both men and women, a careful choice of a good classic blazer and/or suit can pay huge dividends in the years to come. If it really *is* an investment for you, choose a colour that you can jolly up with your accessories: navy blue, which may sound dull, looks great with white, elegant with cream (and will serve as a suitable background to the other kinds of colours which are fashionable one season and passé the next).

For the rest, buy cheap and cheerful things, and trendy high-fashion accessories with a shorter life expectancy. If it gives variety to your wardrobe, and makes it look up-to-date, it doesn't matter if it won't last too long. (*This doesn't apply to special occasion 'outfits'.*)

Shopping should be fun, and the main enjoyment should be from your purchases when you get them home. Do take a friend with you if you really think it'll help; but from my experience 'friends' on shopping sprees can turn out to be just the opposite. A woman who'd brought her friend to my shop couldn't make up her mind between a fabulous feathery confection and a more sober alternative. I wanted her to have the feathery job, and so did she, but the 'friend' said it was quite unsuitable for the occasion. Eventually she left with the more sober alternative and I thought that was the end of it – until 'friend' appeared twenty minutes later and demanded the exotic hat for herself!

As a hat designer I *know* that the right hat can certainly make a woman more beautiful, and I wish more would use hats to enhance themselves. Now I'm not saying a David Shilling hat will do the ironing for you, or that you should buy one instead of a new washing machine. But if you want to give your ego a boost go ahead and buy a hat – you're sure to feel big-headed after the compliments you'll receive. If your ex-boyfriend's getting married, and it should have been to you, nothing will see you through the wedding like a stunning hat.

When you do go out to buy a hat don't be afraid to take your outfit with you. I like a client to try her dress on in my shop and see exactly which shape of hat suits her, and her outfit.

Most people take buying my hats very seriously, but even I was surprised when a well-known singer broke off after fifteen minutes spent on deciding which hat best went with her mink coat to order a new Mercedes by telephone, casually turning to me to ask my opinion on a choice of colours and the shade of the upholstery. All that took no more than four or five minutes; she then continued choosing her hat for a further half hour. (We consider it takes between thirty minutes and an hour to choose a David Shilling hat, even though – or perhaps because – we can make everything in any colour or combination.)

How should you go about putting a 'special occasion' outfit together? In theory, you start with the purchase of the most prominent item first – the suit or the dress – and then work round it. But if you've got the time, when you've found something you really like ask the shop to hold it until you've got your accessories sorted out. I know how difficult it is to buy a hat to go with an outfit if you cannot have one made to order. Even if you're not 'matching' a colour, take the bits of your outfit you've decided on with you – that way, you can be sure they'll work well together. If you're too shy to do this, at least take a swatch of the colours.

Whatever your budget, you should adjust it so you buy the best quality shoes, handbags (and of course, hats) you can afford. It is so sad to see an 'expensive' dress ruined with cheap, bad accessories when someone has obviously invested all their budget on their dress, not on their outfit as a whole, and yet the shoes and bag are at least as important if not more. It's easier to disguise a bad dress using super accessories, than vice versa.

Spend a lot of time choosing, whether or not you've a lot of money. You should never buy clothes you don't really like! There are two types of comfort to consider when you're dressing: the first is physical comfort (if you're wild enough, and love it enough, you might not mind about this) and the second is mental comfort. Make sure you're really comfortable in your clothes before you take them home, and that they're really 'you'.

Smart people never seem to care how they look when they're out. They achieve this not just because they've spent a lot of money on their appearance, but because they've taken enough time to be certain their clothes look good on them. Few things are more ageing than being concerned with your appearance all the time. So another hint is not to take the clothes home and forget about them till it's time to wear them on the big day. Try them on, and get used to them. It's true of high heels, and it's especially true of hats. Put your hat on and do the washing up in it; wear it while you're having a bath (but beware of too much steam). All this will build your confidence. It may sound like a joke, but I really do give my clients this advice. Of course, I'm not sure that all of them do their own washing up, so sometimes I just suggest they walk around the house. I've not yet met the woman so grand that she doesn't do that – although I'm sure there are some, and some who wish they were wheeled around all day.

When you're out shopping, always look at the back view – it's at least half of what you're buying. Men's shops particularly don't provide mirrors so you can see the back – why? After all, you don't just want to see the back of you to see if you look cute – you want to know if the garment fits.

If you're shy of demanding a hand mirror, take a small but suitable one with you on shopping trips just in case.

When you're trying on something don't be too shy to experiment – try a jacket of a suit with a different pair of slacks, pull a skirt length up or down. Alter your hairdo to get the best look for a hat. For most people, it's easiest to choose with all the hair drawn away from the face (unless you'd never actually wear it that way!) and then start experimenting with a little out here and there.

Try and remember if you've seen something similar modelled recently in a magazine. With a hat, was it worn tilted over one eye, worn dead straight forward, or on the back of the head? Try all the variations, anyhow. With a dress, would you like to try it with the collar up, with a tie belt, at the waist or lower, slung on the hip? Roll the sleeves of a jacket up. In other words, stop letting clothes wear you – get in the driving seat and wear them.

I know the assistant won't be thrilled (if you find one to care enough to watch your performance) but they'll be happier to let you experiment than if you bring something back because you didn't like it when you got it home, and they have to give you your money back.

If you want to shop in relative peace, try to go at times when fewer people are around. It's always easiest to shop early in the morning: the shops are usually calm and empty and you get the place to yourself.

Make a phone-call the day before to check opening times – it may be 9, 9.30, or in trendier shops 10 or even 10.30.

Never buy something because you've only got five minutes left to buy it – only buy if it's really what you'd like. If you haven't found something, go home and try to make up an outfit from your existing wardrobe. If extremes are called for, try tying a scarf round your head like a turban, adding lots of jewellery, hitching up a long full skirt to one side and tucking it into a belt cowgirl-style. Try unexpected layers together, a lace blouse over a checked skirt, say, pearls and denim – anything to get you going. The results could be disastrous and inappropriate – but at least they're your clothes and it's free!

If you feel you have to buy something before leaving the shops, buy a pair of shoulder pads – they may give an outfit you've gone off just the lift it needed!

It's never been easier to look good, but because there's a lot of rubbish around – and at all price levels too – the range of choice is almost a drawback. There's too much to choose from. Many women rebelled a decade or two ago against the strictures of 'a fashion': a length of skirt that was 'in' that season, a particular jacket shape or style. Although it cost a little more because you had to buy (and discard) regularly, it did mean a lot of decisions were then made for you.

If you think fashions are expensive now, you should be reminded of what they spent on things a hundred or two hundred years ago! Cashmere shawls were *de rigueur*, and cost as much as a house; lace for centuries was an 'investment' like diamonds or precious jewels. Pearls and gold wire were often used for embroidery on clothes and until cultured pearls came in this century, pearls were worth a fortune. Around the turn of the century feathers for hats were sold for 50 times what you'd get for them today. Osprey and bird of paradise feathers were handed down as heirlooms – now their value is mostly sentimental!

Of course fashion was the prerogative of the few but it was taken very seriously. I have a huge library of fashion journals of the last couple of hundred years. One of the most extraordinary illustrations is from *The Monitor of Fashion:* Ladies' Dress and Patterns for Embroidery for the years 1854-5, and in it a lady wearing a wonderful crinoline is seen with her manservant. The description of the coat, dress and hat is fascinating; the description of the manservant more so.

Equestrian Dress

Olive green pelisse cloth of bombasine, the body cut in the sack form and closed by hooks and eyes up the front, and ornamented with several brooches of turquoise and gold. The sleeve is formed... The skirt is three and a half yards wide and three quarters of a yard longer for walking... The black hat... black veil and dove-coloured gloves... gaiters... boots... complete the dress.

The footman represented is wrongly coloured; he should have curly hair too: for negro footmen are all the rage now, and the blacker the better. We recently received a letter from a gentleman of Paris, requesting us to inform him how to procure a black boy of about sixteen years of age, from this country...

Millinery has always been expensive – a hat appears to have cost about half or a third of the price of a dress, or sometimes more, over the last two or three hundred years. Now it seems nearer a tenth or a fifth, if it's bought at all.

One of my clients, reputedly one of the richest women in the world, found a way of making shopping easier for herself. She would choose her hats, but send her companion (who had exactly the same measurements) for fittings. Because my hats are for special occasions, we try and get everything right – head sizes vary from around $20\frac{1}{2}$ inches to 26 inches, so we make sure our hats fit.

I ask all my clients to bring in not just their dresses, their shoes, their jackets or coats but even their jewels. (This can be quite an experience for me too!) But I need to know if one person's idea of a little pair of diamond and sapphire earrings might be another person's idea of Fort Knox. It's helpful to know if a client wants to wear a favourite piece of jewellery or a special set of jewellery – fussy earrings don't go with cloches. Sometimes we incorporate a jewel in the design of a hat, such as a set of star earrings and small pin on a beret – the perfect gift! Or we make the centre of silk roses with diamond brooches and earclips: I might put a diamond necklace around the base of the crown. I made up one hat which was featured in the *Sunday Express* magazine and it was valued at £100,000.

When brides-to-be come to me with their diamond tiaras it's always a challenge to attach the bridal veils in a suitably modern way, one which respects the jewels but captures today's mood. If the veil is of family lace it's a double challenge to do this without cutting the lace at all. (Some of my clients come to me with their security men. Some even have a bodyguard when they haven't any special jewels with them!)

While we're discussing a hat, I will advise on how the hair should be worn and what make-up to use, especially lipstick. I hate to see this matching a hat; it should always be at least a tone off. In fact, I very seldom make a hat to 'match' an outfit – I usually pick one of the colours and use several tones of the same colour, use shading or a fresh colour entirely to add spice – so a plain navy dress may end up with a hat in white or fuchsia, or with trimmings of several colours.

If you're not having a hat specially made, never buy one that doesn't suit you just because it's got pretty trimmings. Get a hat that does, for it's not too difficult to change the trimmings. Change the colour of the flowers, or add to them to give them more variety; add a bow or some ribbons (not the 'little girl' satin ribbon down the back, if you'd blush at being called 'little girl'). A little steam directed at silk flowers will work wonders if they've been crushed by handling. Go very gently, and avoid the steam going on your straw as it could spoil the shape.

For a very 'country' look, you can even trim your hat with real flowers. Fresh ones won't last long, though, and dried ones tend to be brittle – use a very fine needle to sew them on so as not to split the stems. Half a dozen stalks of natural wheat, dried, look great on the front of the brim of a natural-coloured straw hat. Be careful, because the wheat is very fragile. You could even add some red silk poppies for a splash of colour, and brighten up your outfit, whether it be a blue silk dress, or black and white in one of the numerous 'poppy' prints that are around! Just because it is a natural-coloured straw hat it doesn't have to go with a 'matching' coloured outfit – try interesting contrasts as an alternative.

Make your own clothes. It surprises me that more women don't. Not only do you save money (although many people who make their own clothes spend their budget on more expensive materials, when perhaps if they were buying a ready-made garment they'd buy cheaper, synthetic alternatives), but if you train yourself to be a good dressmaker you'll get a garment at least as well- if not better-finished than some medium-priced outfits. You get the choice of fabrics – even though the shape and detailing on what you make may be dictated to a degree by your skills, or lack of them! If you're not a brilliant dressmaker, choose a pattern that's really simple to make, and spend your time on doing everything with care and attention to detail, even if this means you appear to be getting it done very slowly, and make your fashion statements with the cloth you choose. There are certain garments that anyone should be able to make if they've the patience – for instance a sleeveless T-shirt-shaped summer shift – which could then be accessorized adventurously, and extravagantly sashed around the hips, or given an important belt. But take your time over choosing the fabric – hold it up in the piece and imagine it on you once it is made up. Don't just look for colour and print – will that fabric hang the way you'll want it?

I know a woman with a wonderful figure, so it's not because she can't find anything in her size, who makes all her own clothes although her husband is extremely rich. When she isn't sewing, or helping him in his business, she's jet-setting around the world in her beautiful gowns, and choosing fabulous accessories to go with them.

Finishing touches

Gertrude Lawrence adored jewellery. I was told by someone who knew her that she made a habit of letting her favourite jeweller's shops know which of their wares she'd welcome as a present should any admirer happen to ask them. Apparently, this was not uncommon at the time – other fashionable beauties of stage, screen and society did the same.

She wore her own jewellery on stage, when she felt like it (she was also said to be unpredictable, never giving the same performance twice).

I designed the costumes for *Noel and Gertie*, Sheridan Morley's play with Simon Cadell and Joanna Lumley in the title roles. She floated in on white silk chiffon gaudets on the bottom of a tube of silver-embroidered white satin, and since the action of the play ruled out a change of costume I found her lots of diamanté pieces (including stars for her hair) – to give her the luxury of choosing her jewels for each evening's performance, just as Gertie did.

Men's jewellery is talked about a lot, and designers have a go – but no one seems to wear it. Mine now stays locked up in the bank. While it's a very glamorous idea to have diamond buckles or buttons, who wants to have to go to the bank every morning to get their buttons out? How would you keep your jacket done up until you got there?

But to see a beautiful woman wearing a serious set of jewellery is very exciting, even though it's not usually a beautiful *young* woman who wears the best jewellery. Diamonds, rubies, sapphires and emeralds can be among the benefits of growing older.

If you haven't got good jewellery, it's better not to wear any at all. (It's also better to wear no furs than poor quality.) There's no truth in the rumour that fake is indistinguishable from the real thing. People in the know can tell. Why else would Shirley Bassey have complemented me on that diamond heirloom, at another party, and then offered to swop her pair of diamond earrings for it?

When they're choosing a wedding and engagement ring, most couples hope they're choosing jewellery they will go on enjoying for a very long time. Costume jewellery, all the rage and even worn by women with plenty of the real thing because it's fun, will lose its value as soon as it goes out of fashion; this can be very expensive. A twenty-carat diamond ring may cost £250,000 if it's of good quality and cut, but it's likely to hold (and increase) its worth. The great thing about diamonds is that most people don't mind buying them second-hand.

Too few women realize as they get older that their jewellery may no longer suit them – just like a mini-skirt or jeans; a sweet little Victorian chip diamond ring, or a twenty-first birthday gold animal brooch may have been charming once on a young girl – is it so appropriate now? Small diamonds don't impress people in the know. Maybe you're sentimentally attached to it: you could have it reset if the gems are of sufficient value; there may be times when wearing that piece of jewellery is more appropriate than others. Or it may be time to hand it on to someone who is just the right age for it, as you were once!

The father of one of my best friends at school was in the diamond business and knew I was intrigued by them, and arranged for me to see the diamond later known as the Star of Sierra Leone before it went to auction. I remember arriving at the De Beers headquarters and being escorted past guard after guard till we arrived at a small unassuming office at the end of a long corridor. There, a small cardboard box with sealing wax and string around it, was brought in, and opened with a minimum of procedure. Suddenly, there it was – like a medium-sized lump of coal. But like a lump of coal reproduced with all the individual unique textures each lump has – but in perspex (it was clearer than crystal). Although it weighed around half a pound, it was only two and a half inches across by one and a half; in diamond dealer's terms it was 968.8 carats, and at the time it was the largest single uncut diamond (it was the third largest piece ever found, the Cullinan being the biggest). It was found by a small farmer in his back lot. And I was being asked if I'd like to hold it – and there it was in the palm of my hand – it fitted quite well actually – and I was having a small lecture on how it could be cut up to produce the best combination of fully cut diamonds as we know them, a marquise here, a brilliant there, or an emerald cut. It was quite incredible to be holding in the palm of my hand something that was intrinsically so valuable it was several times what even the greediest amongst us could sensibly expect to win on the pools. It was bought by Harry Winston for an undisclosed amount, and was eventually cut up into eleven fine white diamonds, the largest being 143.2 carats.

Unless you're highly skilled you should avoid making your own jewellery – except for the beach or sunny resorts, when you may be able to concoct exotica with beads and raffia (but it's getting harder and harder to find the old-fashioned kind as it's replaced by plastic), and by adding a few indigenous flowers get a jolly result. Or you could twine ribbons around your pearls or beads to go with an outfit. Otherwise, leave jewellery to the shops, to be bought – preferably by someone else for you!

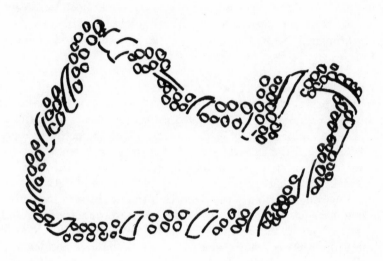

Belts are great around good waists, and trying on an old belt reminds you if you need to watch your weight. As the fashions and the colours in belts change, it seems sensible to buy carefully but cheap. I had a great idea for 'saving' on belts. I had Cartier make me a solid gold buckle, which is very plain, and then I have leather belts made in any colour I want to slip on to it. Nobody would guess it's gold, and this is great because this belt seems to have a life of its own. It never wants to come home with me when I've been staying with people; they're surprised at my enormous pleasure when I get it returned, until I tell them exactly why I'm so grateful.

Of course, don't just think that belts are to be worn around the waist, they can be slung around the hips; or you can add two together. And there's bound to be a revival from time to time of the Sam Browne belt that winds around the shoulder also.

Footwear, tights and stockings are important accessories for women. Next to make-up, they are one of the cheapest ways to put new colour into a look; and at last hosiery manufacturers are offering a lot more than flesh tones – pattern and colour are equally important.

Shoes are a problem because to me the most important thing is to have comfortable shoes. In New York, where women are expected to be ultra-smart in the office, they manage both by travelling to work in sneakers and then changing to formal high heels at work. On one occasion I sat next to Janet Reger at a dinner, and as she kicked off her shoes she told me that she was wearing her highest heels because she'd thought she'd be sitting down for most of the evening – but the reception party before had gone on for so long that her plans had gone awry.

Gloves are little thought about, and yet for evening-wear long black gloves, especially those that come above the elbow and have all those tiny buttons, are terribly sexy and great fun. Apart from that, you don't need them. If you're wearing them to hide something, *leave them on*. When I met the legendary Gloria Swanson I was impressed by the beauty of the small figure, alert eyes and tightened features framed by the black cloche hat worn low over the eyebrows and tight around her face. The rest of her body was draped dramatically and carefully. She wore long black gloves, the highest of collars to cover the neck and her skirt flowed. No spare skin was visible until she suddenly and un-expectedly removed her glove and there the Hollywood legend was totally eclipsed by the memory of that hand, more extraordinary than the face, the disfiguring claw that – for me – outshone the beauty.

Colour is terribly important in my life, as are my friends. You can often tell someone's mood by the colours they're wearing, don't rely on it too much! An intriguing idea is to categorize people one knows into colours: there are too many mentally grey people; life's much more exciting with a few reds around – a little at a time of them is great. Blue people we all know (electric blue could be your code name for a manic depressive). Yellow people are those who come and brighten up your life.

(I don't write a diary, but for anyone who does this might be a better classification, and less embarrassing if the diary were mislaid, than marks out of ten?)

Gifts, toys and playthings

I once designed a range of lingerie which went on sale in Knightsbridge, and when it was shown on 'Pebble Mill at One', it was so
revealing that I am still asked about it. There was an amazing black
chiffon coat printed with a David Shilling design in gold, and worn
over a minute toga that was hard to put on, but very easy to slip off!
The most expensive item was the pure silk dressing gown (floor-length,
with a Japanese-style belt) at around £500. But if you think that's
expensive, I've seen an advertisement in a glossy magazine for a man's
dressing gown which an Old Bond Street shop offers for £2,500. Admit-
tedly, that one's embroidered in gold thread...

The Times asked me, along with two other designers (David Linley
and Caroline Charles) to think up a Christmas gift which anyone, even
a child, could make. This, too, is a dressing gown – and could be made
for around £5. Turn over to find out how.

Perhaps one of the bravest presents a man can buy for a girlfriend is
lingerie. Expensive in effort, even in a chain store. It's claimed that up
to 38 per cent of women's underwear is bought from Marks and
Spencer's, which shows that extravagant underpinnings would be a
treat for lots of people. And it's not such an unselfish gesture for a man
to buy his lady sexy knickers or naughty nighties – after all, he's hoping
he's going to enjoy seeing them worn. (Though the Knightsbridge shop
which sold my range of lingerie did say that quite a surprisingly large
proportion of their stock was bought by men – for themselves!)

If you are feeling shy and have a child to hand (it needn't even be
your own) take the child with you. After all, a man with a child would
hardly... Though most shop assistants don't mind where what they're
selling is going to end up, just so long as you buy something. The best
advice I can give to men wishing to buy underwear as a present is to
decide beforehand what you want to buy and know what you want to
spend, and try to check the sizes you need to buy from the labels of
existing items, which saves worries about trying on.

Materials
Two metres black felt 92 cm wide, two patches of coloured felt 20 cm square (for the pockets), 6 large plastic beads, two metres ribbon 2.5 cm wide in three different colours, four or five ribbons 30 cm long for trimmings, and sequins, beads, shells, feathers, silver foil or whatever you want for further decoration.

Needle
Thread
Pinking shears

Method
1 Fold the felt in half widthways and cut along the centre fold to obtain two oblongs 92 cm × 100 cm. Fold one of these pieces lengthways and cut down fold to obtain two smaller oblongs 46 cm × 100 cm.

2 Use pinking shears all the way round every edge to serrate.

3 Lay the large (92 cm × 100 cm) oblong flat, taking 100 cm as the length. Then position the two smaller pieces on top to cover it exactly. Sew along the top edge from each corner, leaving a gap of 26 cm for the neck. The seams should be about 2 cm from the top of the serrations.

4 Leaving a gap of 31 cm lengthways from the shoulder, sew down each side, stopping 23 cm above the hem to leave a slit.

5 Pink the edges of the coloured patches for the pockets. Fold over the top 5 cm and secure with a couple of stitches on each side.

6 Attach one pocket to the right front about 11 cm above the hem. Stitch the bottom and both sides of the patch to the body fabric, leaving the top of the patch open.

7 Attach the other pocket to the left front in the same way, but position it lower down.

8 Plait the three coloured ribbons together to make a belt. Knot the ends and leave tassels.

9 Trim the left shoulder with the shorter (30 cm) ribbons and whatever else you've got.

Anyone can make this kimono. I do feel strongly it should be in black – children tend to go a bit wild with the trimmings, but multicolours will still look smart on a black background.

If a pony's the perfect gift for the perfect little girl, how about a racehorse as a gift for a bigger girl who's got everything? Or perhaps a share in one?

A twelfth share in a reasonable hurdler could cost around £500, but the upkeep might be around £50 a month. And the owner of a share in such a horse should expect to find herself rubbing shoulders not with dukes or film stars, but more probably with taxi-drivers, greengrocers or miners.

For a real chance at Cheltenham you'd need much nearer £1,000 and for a real chance at Royal Ascot you could need as much as £100,000 for that twelfth share, and proportionally more for upkeep. Of course, the rewards are greater too. Nijinsky is now commanding a $650,000 stud fee (it's rumoured this could reach $1 million in 1987), but the father of Nijinsky, Northern Dancer, is reputed to cover sixty mares in the three-month season for a fee of $1.5 million a time. This is perhaps why the Claiborne stud is reported to have insured its sixteen stallions for $1,000,000,000. (That puts a bet of a fiver each way into perspective!)

It depends where you holiday, but for the person who has 'everything', a foreign version of Monopoly is fun. I like playing with the Champs Elysées one week, Fifth Avenue the next, so I often bring home sets to give away.

The most extravagant gift I think I've ever heard of was when a man came into my shop and asked me to embroider a scarf with initials – not his girlfriend's, but the registration letters of an aeroplane. The silk scarf was just to introduce the main gift, which he intended to present her with at a surprise birthday party.

Of course, we all know with gifts that it's the thought that counts. And most of us would agree with this sentiment – especially when we're doing the giving. I was rather horrified to hear that a famous London chocolatier (the Duke of Edinburgh is said to buy his favourites there) has started a birthday book system: busy people can go in and order all the presents they need to send during the year and the shop will do the rest! Well, if I received chocolates from there I'm not sure I'd feel so flattered to know that someone remembered my June birthday way back in January! I'd rather receive just a card, as long as that person has thought about it and signed it themselves! I must admit I have a system which works for me: I write all my letters and cards personally – but to save time the envelopes are always addressed for me. But I do think that writing by hand personal things like birthday cards, messages of congratulations and thanks is the least you can do – and my way it needn't take too long. Even when I send flowers I try to sign the card personally. Gifts should have a surprise element. It's fun to give diamonds presented in boxes of chocolates, though I admit it would be easy to swallow the size of diamond I give without even noticing.

Gifts on a budget needn't be tacky, and you needn't resort to re-cycling gifts that have been given to you and which you don't want – that's a dangerous game to play. I don't do it any more, since I once caused a terrible insult to someone by giving them something dreadful that I'd forgotten they'd given me! Now these 'gifts' end up at jumble sales, with, I'm afraid I have to admit, not much more charitable motives. There are just a few friends who are responsible for giving the lie to the expression 'something's better than nothing' – nothing would be better than a white porcelain flying pig, or a single simple corn on the cob dish, and a few other atrocities I've received.

If you don't want to spend much you must be a little inventive (although is a couple of pounds too much? For this you can get a bottle of white plonk and that's always acceptable; tie a ribbon round the neck or wrap in cooking foil to make it festive and thoughtful-looking – rather than leaving it in its supermarket bag). Of course the latest trendy gift ideas for the person who has 'everything' have been singing telegrams. The first one I saw was poolside at the Four Seasons about eight years ago – now they get everywhere. You could always do a DIY version. Dress up as something extraordinary – you know the sort of thing – as a Tarzan or Jane, a strippagram. Prepare a little song – new words with relevance set to the tune of a popular song – and off you go, or simply tie a ribbon around yourself, attach a large label and present yourself as the gift. Less embarrassing and less demanding is the more recent balloon in a box, which is literally that. Companies will arrange for a helium-filled balloon to be posted to your friend and it floats up when the box is opened. It really wouldn't be much more of a let-down if you did this yourself by posting an ordinary air-filled balloon in a box, and you'd save several pounds.

Chocolates are nearly always acceptable. I once had a girlfriend whose father was a diamond merchant, but what I liked best about her was that she arranged to have Belgian chocolates flown over for me every week. I kept them in the fridge, and so each batch lasted till the next lot arrived.

A usually generous friend found herself a bit short of money at Christmas time, so she made boxes of truffles as presents for us all – with a bit of help, she managed to make 900! They were wonderful, we were all delighted, and at the present time she and her husband are about to buy a recording studio – not, I imagine, on what she saved from her Christmas presents budget – but I suppose every little bit counts!

I'll give you the recipe. There are apparently certain problems making 900 truffles at a time not encountered when making smaller quantities. I include here the full recipe given to me by my friend – but of course you could make a small quantity if you like. Make up in three batches.

900 Rum Truffles

30 tablespoons instant coffee
15 lb plain chocolate
7½ lb butter
60 tablespoons rum, or other
**   alcohol (1 bottle and a bit)**
Coatings

Dissolve the coffee in about an equal quantity of water.

Break up the chocolate and melt in a large bowl over boiling water (takes quite a while because of the quantity).

When melted take off heat and stir to cool.

Cut up butter into small dice, and stir them into chocolate.

Add rum gradually.

Put mixture into freezer until firm. (If you've only a fridge you'll have to leave till next day. Even in freezer it could take 2–3 hours or longer!)

Now roll chocolate into small balls. (A melon scoop should, but doesn't, work!) Take a teaspoonful at a time and shape by hand.

To stop the mixture melting, coat your hands with icing sugar and keep washing your hands under cold water to keep them cool.

When the mixture you're using gets too soft/warm use an alternate batch.

After they're all in balls, coat in either chopped or ground nuts, or in chocolate vermicelli (but not sugar strands); or dip into melted white or plain chocolate. To do this place one ball at a time on the end of a toothpick! (Not easy, but this was the best method!)

Now put them all into sweetcases and store in airtight boxes, either tins or plastic containers. They keep for months if cool. My friend left hers in the garden all winter! They could last eight months or more.

To serve at room temperature, remember to take them out of the garden a couple of hours before you want to eat them!

The most extravagant Christmas dream I've had was fulfilled when I was asked to decorate a Christmas tree for a feature in *Harpers & Queen* 1984 Christmas issue. I knew that Peter Blake, the artist, was dressing one in classic Victorian style, and that someone else was doing one in white and gold. Wouldn't it be wonderful, I thought, for the tree to sparkle with jewellery? Diamonds, sapphires, emeralds and rubies – a million pounds' worth at least...

I ordered a twisted conifer to make my tree look still more interesting, and for security reasons it was decided it should be trimmed in the boardroom above Cartier's shop in New Bond Street. Once the five-foot-high tree was set up, I set about decorating it with the help of Cosima Fry. Here a diamond necklace, there a dangling earring. A whole tray of pearl necklaces were brought in and draped over the branches. The photographer, assistant, security man all stood by as the gems were piled on – the finishing touch was to be a white replica dove, with a large ring round its neck.

We had almost finished when suddenly we heard that Paul McCartney was in the shop, and we were asked to take off several essential pieces. Slowly, more and more of the decorations disappeared until he finally settled on a single ring; we could begin trimming again.

Finally we stood back. If ever there was a money tree, I hope it would look as pretty as this.

Give flowers, with a difference; everyone loves orchids, and they exude a feeling of luxury. A gift of orchids is always a delight, from the little sprays which when in season are great value at £1 or £2 (display them a single stem at a time in narrow glass vases; you could even make up a small collection of four or five champagne flutes as orchids often come in bunches of four or five, and put one in each flute), to the glorious large and exotic orchids. These can be arranged in any charming container, it needn't be a vase. Some glass food jars are ideal for flower arranging – though with some you simply can't disguise the fact they weren't born to a life of flower showing but were born 'working class'! I don't normally like orchids worn pinned on a dress; don't ever wear a corsage to the theatre, whatever your age. If you want to wear flowers, wear them in the hair, over one ear, or a spray across one side of the head and trailing around the back, or even an entire circlet. The younger you are, or the more extrovert, the more exotic you could make the arrangement.

Back to orchids. For a really splendid orchid gift how about giving an orchid plant – perfect for the woman who has everything. Of course, orchids are difficult to grow; order a plant in bloom from a well-known

florist. (Orchids may not always be in stock, and they are in season at all different times.) However, if you want to teach your loved one that with care things grow – and beautifully – why don't you contact an orchid grower and seek advice before buying a plant, or several plants, that could have every chance of surviving at least as long as or even longer than your relationship will! Although many orchids love humidity and lots of light and being raised in greenhouses, lots thrive indoors if under the supervision of someone who's good with normal houseplants. Perhaps the most decadent way I've seen orchids growing is from hanging baskets, which I normally don't like. This would be almost impossible to achieve in the English climate – but it certainly beats geraniums.

Some orchid single blooms last for as long as ten weeks or more, and for many their flowering period extends throughout the winter. Cool growing orchids can be grown in temperatures as low as 10°C/50°F.

Growers think most plants seem to like rainwater better than tapwater. I was particularly advised to only give rainwater to the carnivorous plant I ordered at the Chelsea Flower Show one year. I was so intrigued by their weird shapes and wonderful markings that I chose the names of them for a whole collection of hats. (Sadly, mine died. I don't know whether it objected to cocktails of rain- and distilled water, or whether my house didn't offer enough red meat.)

I spotted an unusual arrangement in my local florist's, Richards and Hughes: two china dogs and a couple of plants arranged tree-like on a platter of moss. It was to be a birthday gift from one canine to another!

Toys for men are specialized – pipes, tennis rackets, golf clubs – but the most obvious universal male toy is the motor car.

We all know that to us our car is a Rolls Royce, and we all know that nobody who really owns a Porsche ever has a sticker on an old banger telling you so. But what fewer people realize when they're driving their Fiat Unos or Minis or Golfs, aspiring to a Rolls or Ferrari, is that a lot of people who have these drive around the city in much humbler vehicles because it's easier. So you can easily improve the status of your car for less than the price of a tank of four-star. Next time you drive your modest car – and I hope you're not driving at the moment because you need a hand to turn over the pages and whoops! watch that corner, it's sharper than you thought – drive it as though you were enjoying the freedom from the restriction of the Rolls, which needs so much space to park and about which you must be so careful because a scratch can cost thousands, a hub-cap lost costs hundreds of pounds to replace, and if the Silver Lady mascot is stolen – which happens often, my father had four stolen last year – it's maddening.

Of course, you can buy a secondhand Rolls – and a twenty-year-old

one is not likely to set you back more than a brand new full-price
saloon – but to my mind the real pleasure of owning a Rolls would be
choosing all the refinements, such as the colour of the upholstery, the
wood on the dashboard, and knowing that you have a car as nearly
suited to your individual wishes as possible, and at the same time one of
the world's great classic status symbols. A Phantom VI, the largest and
most luxurious model, will cost between £200,000 and £250,000,
depending on the extras you want; but you could get a Rolls or a
Bentley and have enough change out of a third of that amount to insure
it and fill the tank a few times.

Owning a Rolls Royce isn't going to give you style instantly – but many people will be impressed. Others, though, may think you're the chauffeur (if you're young enough, this might even add to your attraction), and more cynical members of the public may dismiss it as on H.P., and 'nouveau'. (Better nouveau than 'never'.) It is true that a Rolls Royce is one of the easiest stylish assets you can acquire if you've the money (and if there isn't too long a waiting list for the model you're after). It takes some sensitivity to choose antique silver or a good collection of paintings, and a wonderful house will cost an awful lot more in upkeep.

I'm only impressed by old marques, and it seems that the most fashionable cars are old ones.

Since I hate driving long distances myself, and walk to work, I need a car that's easy to park, and because I tend to go fast if the car can, it's safer if it can't! I adore my Mini-moke. I knew I would, even before I bought it.

I hadn't driven for a while when a girlfriend (now ex) gave me an old Deux Chevaux for my birthday (I think she thought this might reduce my love of being driven, which it didn't). It was good fun to drive, the best fun being when it almost blew up. I was on my way to a friend's from a drinks party, where two old dears had looked a little lost when they were introduced to me, and so I'd introduced them to each other – only to find they'd been living together for fifty years. I can recognize a suitable match when I see one (after all, Dolly, the matchmaker of *Helly Dolly!* was a milliner, I'm often reminded – although the milliners of days gone by were far more bawdy – men knew there was more to tickle their fancy at most hat shops last century than the odd feather or two).

By the time I got to my friends' house at Hampstead's Vale of Health, there was smoke coming from the bonnet. Their large house is fronted by a huge garden with a high wall all round. I parked hastily and ran out. I was casually dressed in sneakers and a white cotton boiler suit with black zips. It had been a gorgeous sunny day, it was a perfect English summer evening and when Gillian said come round I'd expected a light supper in the garden. I should have known better, I'd known her since my teens, before she even married Maurice Saatchi and now she was separated. (She has since become Mrs Davis.)

As I flung open the gates and started shouting for help I was greeted by the sight of at least a dozen formally-clad dinner guests sipping cocktails and ignoring my entrance as another bit of show-off theatre – especially as I was not only wearing less formal clothing but less of it! It took several minutes to convince them what was happening, by which time the cloud of smoke enveloping my Citroën could be seen above the garden wall. The fire brigade had been called by a neighbour and arrived with the police; not only were most of the locals out to witness the 'fun', but one woman started haranguing me that I was poisoning her babies – totally untrue but what could I have done had it not been?

Over dinner Gillian kindly offered me a choice of their cars – they had extras in the garage! I chose a Mini-moke and when I'd driven it for a day or two I knew that was the car I wanted. I shortly found one for sale – nineteen years old. But it happened to be owned by a decorator who'd kept it at his holiday house in the Canaries and he was a best friend of Prince Stefano Massimo (the son of Dawn Addams, a great photographer of many of my hats, and a close friend).

I didn't expect all this pedigree to make the car go faster but it did make me take a chance on an elderly vehicle that had long since been given up by the vicar's wife!

Only one other vehicle has given me real pleasure. That was the tricycle, described correctly as 'such an elegant machine'. It was built by Condor in Gray's Inn Road and had ten-speed gears. It got me from Regent's Park to Lloyd's in the City faster than colleagues could do it in their Ferraris – we tried the race several times – and didn't cost as much to park. Bicycles were charged 20p and cars £2.00. I felt I was getting good value when I suggested I'd pay 30p to use the Members' Garage – after all it was a three-wheeler!

In L.A. cars are collected much as antiques are here. A friend has a garage on the side of his house which all his guests are expected to visit and there in pristine condition, all gleaming like silver sports cups, are his cars, which include a gull-wing Mercedes, and of course, in pride of place, a Bentley. Another friend who collected Bugattis had one as the centrepiece of his Los Angeles drawing room, as he considered it as beautiful as any sculpture, but after six months he moved it out because of the smell of oil. To me, cars are for getting from A to B even if it is in style! I don't even find aeroplanes exciting; fortunately I've yet to see one of those in somebody's living room – although Roger Daltrey does have one at the bottom of the garden, and not far away are his helicopters.

The first time I went up in a micro-light it was with Roger Daltrey. He made an incredible fuss about me wearing a safety helmet and lent me a sheepskin-lined leather jacket so that I looked like a cross between something out of *The Dam Busters* and *Easy Rider*! It had no cabin as such, you just sit on a bucket seat suspended beneath the wings; the petrol is in a tank not much more substantial than those large plastic jerrycans you get orange squash in; and your feet rest on two small metal plates. Whoosh, you rise pretty steeply and the view around and below you is incredible, but I must admit suddenly at 1,000 feet up I was seized by an extraordinary feeling that all the fuss about the crash helmet was somewhat unnecessary! (As they said in *Butch Cassidy*: 'I can't swim!' '*Swim*?! The fall'll probably kill you.') Being with a member of the British rock group most famous for smashing up their musical instruments didn't help add to my confidence. As we landed, and it felt just like that, I've never seen grass come towards me so quickly!

Other status toys are electronic: electric gates and garage doors are fun for owners and guests, though you tend to feel a bit silly the first time you talk to a small box on a metal pole and ask it to open the gates to let you into the driveway. (Remember when you're leaving to give them enough room to open, as some swing back towards you.) You can even open your car doors electronically by remote control, and cars even tell you the temperature outside. (Do you really need to be reminded if it's 'minus' in winter?)

Then there are mobile phones. When they first came out I had one, and then changed to a supposedly superior model, but I never found them terribly reliable. They were good for a few surprised looks in restaurants and on the beach! They've now become quite common-place, and in cars seem to attract thieves – but at least with these new models you can hold a two-way conversation without all the 'over' and 'roger' business that the early ones attracted because only one of you had the airwaves at once. (For me, it's not a luxury to have a telephone, but to *not* have one. Which is why there are sockets all over my house, but very few actual receivers.)

What would be the gift I'd most like to receive? A magazine once asked me what I wanted for Christmas, and I told them, honestly, 'World peace.' 'Yes,' they persisted, 'but *personally*, what would you like?' I replied, 'Jet-skis.' The article was published, but I'm still waiting for either to turn up!

Gold-diggers' guide

*Y*ou might think it's very hard to get a public image, but remember Andy Warhol's claim that *everyone* is a star – for at least 15 minutes of their life. Obviously, there are stars and there are *stars*. How can you get a foot on the ladder to the realms of gold?

Television makes instantaneous stars out of quiz show contestants, or people simply picked at random in the street for their views, or even chance witnesses to crime. Those ways apart, it's probably easiest to become well-known on the next rung of the ladder by being 'bad', and you're more likely to stay there as long as you continue. There are a lot of Old Etonians, sons of peers, top sportsmen and soap opera heroes, who are notorious because they once stepped out of line, generally with one of the dailies' three D's: divorce, drunken driving, or drugs. The trouble is, once you've got the reputation, you're always good for a story. The cow who jumped over the moon is never going to be allowed to forget her feat. Jack Spratt is obviously the world's most famous anorexic. As far as the media are concerned, once 'bad', always bad. They are always looking for a simple hook for their stars. If you want your name in the papers, it helps if you're related to someone famous, titled, or rich. If you're a girl, and beautiful, being seen once or twice with the right man will help. But the newspapers want new faces, so if you're photographed with too many men too quickly, you'll just appear to be a slut. A man isn't going to get photographed at all unless he's devastatingly handsome, and even then it helps if he's with a beautiful or interesting woman. Newspaper picture editors tend to be men!

So if you don't want to be bad, or aren't content just to be a quiz show contestant, how do you become famous? If you're not prepared, like Margaret Thatcher, to spend years getting to the top, being a pop star or acting are the fast areas in the Eighties. Modelling isn't what it was, nor is hairdressing. (In fact, hat-making seems to have ousted these last two recently but even that might be on the decline, so many are jumping on the hat-band wagon!)

Designers in general are getting more status. Photographers are still much photographed. Then there are mini-stars – interviewers, even weather people, cooks and health experts. It's up to you and your talent to get noticed – and, if you've got no talent, to hide that fact.

One talented man I knew who was a great inspiration and encouragement to me was the late Sir Cecil Beaton. I remember vividly leaving a packed theatre after seeing Maggie Smith in *Hedda Gabler*:

milling crowds tried to get out, filling the foyer. Slowly the side entrances cleared, but Cecil Beaton waited to make his exit with a flourish through the centre – a star makes a statement whether it's an entrance or an exit!

You may find yourself in the vicinity of stars and popping flashbulbs. If your photograph is taken for use in a magazine, do wait for the photographer to ask for your name. You can then ask what publication it's for (though it's smarter not to). Don't be too optimistic – having your photograph taken doesn't automatically mean it will be used. In the world of newspapers there are busy days and slow ones: there are days when they can do with a photo of a bird at a local cat show – on other days a Cabinet Minister's resignation is relegated to page 7!

We've all dreamed of marriage to a prince or princess one day, and living happily ever after. There are many ways to meet and marry a millionaire/millionairess – but do you really want to? I remember seeing the play *Trafford Tanzi*, about the battle of the sexes – played out in a wrestling ring. It ended with Tanzi's husband battling against her because she was now the breadwinner and he didn't want to do the household chores. Of course, if he landed a multi-millionairess, no man would even have to bother about doing the housework himself! But stop and think – millionaire or millionairess – do you really want to? It could be an expensive way of earning your money. In theory, when you sue for divorce you end up with a packet. Beware. Those who always end up with a lot of money are the lawyers – even the estate agents. The reports of multi-multi-million dollar settlements are as few and far between as gold strikes and many are as unfounded in fact, and many ex-wives of hugely wealthy men have found so to their cost.

Suppose you're due for a million pounds, you think. Think again, and halve or third that million. People divorcing are mean; and how did your ex get the money in the first place? Having got it, most people intend keeping it. You've probably got another 40 years ahead of you, so divide your half or third of a million by that: £8,500, even £12,500, a year doesn't sound so good, does it? A 21-year-old friend of mine earns that much, is being trained to use computers *and* gets the weekends off.

Any seriously rich man is probably in love with his work. Are you prepared to take second place to that? If you surmount that hurdle, you'd better check out the prospective mother-in-law, *and* check that

The author's home photographed by James Mortimer: the entrance hall

The author's home: the drawing room from opposite aspects

Mrs Gertrude Shilling, wearing gold and flame brocade with ostrich feathers

his castle's got central heating! Of course, you may find a young charming good-looking multi-millionaire, or maybe one who's just unlucky enough to have become a widow – but these are rare. If he's unattached, look in his cupboard for skeletons of quite a different nature.

The trouble with looking for love is that you wait around for ages, and just like buses, three turn up all at once. Like policemen, you can never find a rich man when you really need one.

My advice would be that if you're prepared to spend the time and energy on marrying money, you'd probably be better advised to use that energy from the start on making it for yourself. But if you still think the other way's better, here are a few tips – things to do and places to be.

One way to meet rich people is house-hunting. If you've a fabulous home, you just need to ring an estate agent and put it on the market for a highly inflated figure that would interest a millionaire or two. Trouble is you're likely to get a lot of gold-diggers coming round too, and a lot of representatives of the rich looking on their behalf. It's probably easier in the long run actually to do the house-hunting yourself. Dress up: if you've a Rolex watch and some Louis Vuitton, it's enough to impress an estate agent – with these, you can wear jeans. But otherwise for her a good fur would be appropriate, suit for him. Your price range should be high – $£\frac{1}{2}$ million at least, if not more – choose your location and do a little bit of homework. How many bedrooms do you want, can you expect a swimming pool in that area and price range. Then don't be fobbed off by videos and photos, let them get you out on the road! So be vague, even mysterious. If you don't feel you can get away with being the purchaser yourself, claim either that you've just been left a large sum of money or that it's being bought for you by mummy or daddy – nobody will believe it but that will stop them asking any more questions.

By the way, don't overlook the estate agent, especially if he/she is very young! He may have been put there to learn the ropes by a father who's also in the business and is using the opportunity to spy on the opposition. If you get the opportunity to check out their credentials, what have you got to lose? When you go round the homes make sure you're with the owners, not some surrogate by simply saying what a lovely home you've got, etc. If this doesn't get the information you need – be more direct.

Fetching the kids from school is an especially good approach for guys. 'Borrow a brat' to take to or from the most expensive private school you know, and smile at all parents of opposite sex. You may have to do this regularly at first, but soon you'll find out the lonely ones and those who are, or are about to be, divorced. One sight of their cars should tell you whether you've hit a jackpot or not. If not, ask 'your' child about the other child – kids are much more direct about these things. Little Tommy's house is bigger than ours, Lizzie's daddy drives a Rolls Royce. They've got an au pair!

The other most obvious way is to try an exclusive nightclub, if you're reasonably attractive; go for anyone at a table with champagne buckets. Once you're in the group, try finding out who's paying for it all. Don't be surprised if it's a famous hairdresser or footballer, though. The trouble with this idea is that apart from Annabel's in London, Castel in Paris and the Mike Todd room (which is almost an exclusive club within the already reasonably exclusive Palladium) in New York, the most successful nightclubs are one-nighters. The facilities of an established club are taken over for one night of the week; the cognoscenti get to know immediately through an extraordinary grapevine, but once too many people know, it moves on. Taboos, for instance, which was Thursdays at Maximus in Leicester Square, started going downhill when the first film-makers arrived, and closed the same week as a four-page spread appeared in a Sunday colour supplement. Now the 'hottest' club is the Café de Paris, on Wednesdays. One night recently George Michael, Bill Wyman, a Duranie, Paul Rutherford of Frankie were there, drinking Pils to the Bossa Nova. The next week Tina Turner and Andy Warhol turned up, but paparazzi on the way out indicated this club soon will be too!

The problem for the gold-digger at such a club is the chameleon tendency of anyone rich or famous, who will blend in so perfectly that they appear outstanding only because of their total ordinariness. So either go for someone whose face makes you think you've seen it before – or the tattiest leather jacket in the place. If it doesn't ask you to borrow 10p – it could be worth £10m.

Rule number one of courtship: Van Cleef and Arpels First; Lust later.

So, once you've met your friend, how do you know if they're going to match your ideals? Too often I've seen girls go after men for money, and still be unmarried ten years later and lucky to have a rabbit's foot let alone a mink coat!

Find out if he's/she's mean. Basically, if you're sent one rose after the first date, don't be fooled – this is not a romantic sign. It's cheaper than a bunch! So, it's about time you had a birthday. Choose any day (make sure you know the birth sign though – and if it's Virgo or Leo the birthstone too – these two are diamonds and sapphires). If the gift and entertainment laid on aren't lavish enough, you've got to start again.

Birthdays are in fact frightfully useful for the gold-digger. If you're not getting the love and attention (and the wedding ring) that you think you deserve, in six months time have another birthday. If he, or she, asks 'Didn't you have one six months ago?' instead of showering you with gifts, you know it's time to cut out. Or you could keep telling him, or her, how clever it is of Piaget to put 87·87 carats of diamonds into a teenzy-weenzy watch and charge around one million dollars – and clock the reaction!

The only other use for birthdays is when you're in an Italian or Greek restaurant. If it's *really* your birthday you can let them know in advance, but even if it isn't your birthday, tell them it is. It's no crime and they'll enjoy it just as much as you. In fact, if you've a friend who's a bit down in the dumps arrange it without telling him or her first. This gives quite a new meaning to the expression 'surprise birthday party'. As a general rule, though, birthdays have no other use after you're 21! Forget them, they're nasty things and do nobody much good.

Expensive shops and hotels are great places to meet the rich. A shop like Asprey's in Bond Street is an especially good place, particularly around Christmas because they have such a wide variety of prices that you can be idly considering the purchase of a corkscrew, whilst keeping an eye on the adjacent antique jewellery counter. Even if you have to buy something occasionally, it needn't cost you the earth. Fortnum & Mason is packed with potential, if you sift through the tourists, and you won't find you've chatted up the staff by mistake – they all wear tailcoats.

In top hotels you may find you have to spend money, but that doesn't mean you've got to take the most expensive suite. I'd always recommend staying in the humblest room in the grandest hotel, rather than the best suites in the second best, because you still get to share all the same amenities, the pools, the bars, the restaurants, etc... although if you're charming, polite and suitably dressed these should seldom be barred to you anyway.

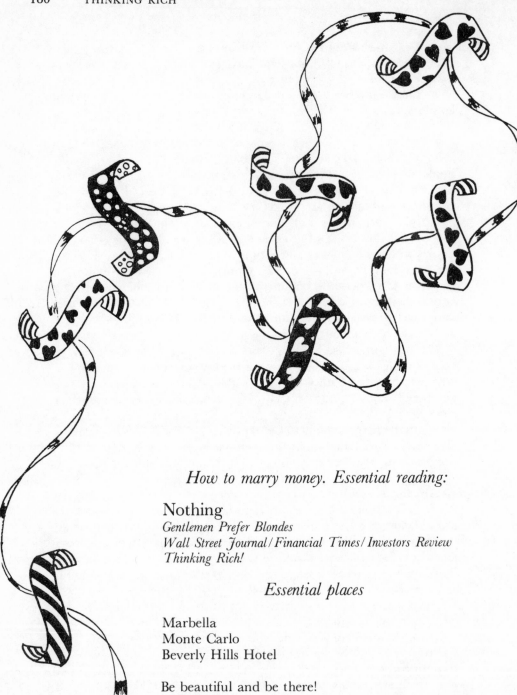

How to marry money. Essential reading:

Nothing
Gentlemen Prefer Blondes
Wall Street Journal / Financial Times / Investors Review
Thinking Rich!

Essential places

Marbella
Monte Carlo
Beverly Hills Hotel

Be beautiful and be there!

Being Rich and Famous involves what? Being rich means having accountants, solicitors, tax advisers, insurance brokers, stockbrokers, endless lunches with bankers, and each freedom gained is another lost. Not many rich men are actually that famous – they'd probably say they don't want to be, but they haven't got the time anyhow! And many 'famous' people aren't rich because it costs them a lot to remain famous.

Fame has its drawbacks, too. I have a distant cousin, who's a drummer in a rock band. He has to keep moving house, as whenever fans find his address it becomes impossible to stay there. Of course, this won't go on for ever – and that can almost be worse. (If you're famous, you can't give out your phone number too freely – unless you are prepared to keep changing that too.)

To appear rich doesn't mean you have to spend a lot of money, you just have to appear to have lots of it. Anyone with a silk suit and a gold watch can appear rich if they play the rest of the game well! The richer you are, quite often the more people are willing to pay your expenses. One wheeze is to have the largest denomination of currency on you (at present you can, for instance, get Scottish £100 pound notes which are quite legal in England). You'll never be able to get change for that for a small round of drinks or a taxi fare.

If you want to save money, don't carry a coat or umbrella. That saves you the embarrassment of a tip, saved every time you don't have to check them in. You don't have to decide whether as a 'rich' person you have to give a huge tip – or a tiny one! Never walk to your table in a restaurant wearing your fur; it looks as if you've only just got it.

If people try to tell you that stars are the same as everybody else – don't believe it. Most of them do have an indefinable magic – some are confident, others shy; for some, success just drops on to their plates, others appear helpless but they have worked like hell for it! There's no one quality that will bring you success. But you can pick up some tips on that Star quality. For instance, Jill Bennett really impressed me once by putting her telephone number on a cheque and signing it with her usual aplomb! I also know people who jot things down on banknotes, using them as free notepaper – though you never know who's going to read those notes eventually.

One of the things you must learn is that famous and rich people kiss a lot; stars especially, often as much as four times on meeting and again, seconds later, when they 'must go and see someone over there'. If you're unaccustomed to this, you'll have to practise with a friend so as to avoid getting your ears chewed off, or, if you're fond of your earrings, how to avoid getting them mangled or, worse still, losing them. A star won't be too happy with a faceful of your best diamanté either! Incidentally, practise this under a hat too.

Yes, stars do wear sunglasses a lot – especially male British actors renowned for their eyes. They tend to choose shades to add mystery and a little colour, thus highlighting the eyes rather than obliterating them altogether – and also helping shade the earliest signs of wrinkles. A lightly-tinted pair of sunglasses does let the eyes relax whatever light you're in, so they must be good news if you're afraid of getting crows' feet. If you're a star, it's all right for you to wear sunglasses whenever you like. Just be careful, if you don't want this to cost a fortune, to remember to put them back on when you're wearing them. I'm always losing masses of sunglasses. Mercifully, now it's fashionable to wear cords round the neck. I have them in masses of colours and this has temporarily stemmed the losses! Young stars wear Raybans, older ones wear Porsche (that's pronounced Pors*her*) and older women stars still wear large ones with designer initials.

You can butter up the person you're attracted to and have them for breakfast, using almost any wile you want, but don't start name-dropping unless you're on strong ground. It's a tiny world and even if you're abroad a really heavyweight name is likely to get you into really heavyweight trouble. The greater the name you drop, the more everyone will make an effort to prove they know them at least as well, and you may soon find yourself out of your depth! Also name-dropping internationally is quite an art because so many British 'stars' are quite unknown abroad, or are better loved, say, in France than in the US. The husband of a well-loved musical comedy star once said to me with honesty about her, 'She's huge in Scunthorpe.' This may have been true, and she's known in London's West End too, but I'd doubt you'd be offered a nickel for her most intimate secrets in Minnesota or Maine.

In fact stars are often more vulnerable than you'd think. I've heard of a star who got her secretary to go out and buy someone a present, wanted to see that she approved of it – did, but then had it sent back to Cartier for them to gift-wrap it!

You must never ask actors what they're doing at the moment. In fact, with unemployment worldwide it's probably safer not to ask anyone, 'What do you do?' This will avoid potential embarrassments. At one end of the scale someone might have just lost a job, and at the other end, might be so rich as simply not to need to work. Even worse than that, you might be asking someone famous and the ego might not be able to stand it. I remember a fabulous dinner in the South of France thrown into disarray when an Italian (I think she was a Contessa) asked a very handsome and well-respected English actor what he did, whereupon he put down his napkin and scuttled off! I'm still not certain whether she was teasing, but I have to admit I rather admire the cheek of both of them.

You must also remember not to ask an actor where he's been, just because he's got a suntan, and this too is a word of warning with a fairly general application. It's as likely to have been no further than the local sun bed parlour as somewhere exotic, and many people even have them at home!

You mustn't be too reserved, so go ahead and say what else you like; they say that those who matter don't mind and those who mind don't matter. Although I've witnessed some fairly fabulous 'minding'. Over lunch, one girl told another that she ought to have plastic surgery on her eyes. 'I prefer my maid' was the reply, tempered by the addition, as an afterthought, 'You must have thought I was 19.' On another occasion, a man turned to someone boasting about a watch with two dials, one set for time in his London office, one his New York office. 'You're not on foreign time, you're on borrowed time!'

A friend of mine was dismissive of one mutual acquaintance, 'She wears her skirts two inches longer than her mink coat,' and of another, who'd got into an unsuitable relationship, 'Her dining room table is too big for his dinner parties.'

Rich is an attitude, it isn't an amount in your bank account. One man's nightmare is another man's wife! You can live a rich life on less, or be unhappy counting your millions. Of course the best things in life aren't all free, but many of them are accessible or affordable and you should always be able to give yourself some cheer at not much expense. If someone asks you if you've a yacht, say, 'No, not at the moment.' If you're an insomniac you can cheer yourself up at no extra cost by counting mink coats rather than sheep.

If you break an arm or leg it's a great opportunity for you to meet new friends, not just nurses and doctors, but you can ask people to autograph your plaster, or you could put a simple message on it, like 'Hello!' and wait for the fun to begin.

Most people don't realize how close they come to living a life of luxury. It's not a matter of money – it doesn't cost much to throw a teaspoon of brandy over a dessert and make it a flambé, and if we made one less telephone call a day we would all have the time to put aside to improve our bodies with a few exercises.

Luxury is, of course, relative – on a cold day there is no greater luxury than a hot cup of tea, on a hot day a cool can of beer or a Coke. The trouble is that most of us in the developed world are so surrounded by it in our daily lives, we take it for granted – so it's no longer a luxury! A childlike attitude here may be envied rather than pitied. Children can close their eyes and for an instant think they're anywhere they want to be. As adults, some of us are too lazy to get out of our seats to enjoy a beautiful tree in blossom or a flower bursting into bloom; or too vain to share the enjoyment of someone else's achievement or a colleague's good fortune. A luxury can be a cool breeze in a tropical climate, or mulled wine after a brisk winter's walk.

Feeling rich is a state of mind. Why else do we think of Robin Hood and his Merry Men as being 'rich' (and with only one girl between them, and her Robin's?) Find yourself a fountain, throw a coin in and make a wish. So what if it doesn't come true? You won't have lost much by it. Go to a perfume shop and try the testers. Plan a lecture or a recital – in a crowded bus if there's nowhere else. Get an old dinner jacket and decorate it, perhaps with splashes of paint, or with glitter and beads – even do a 'his' and 'hers' look (she could wear hers with a swimsuit, and so could he, but shorts or cut-offs are possibly more appropriate). Simply remind yourself it's good to be alive!

However, if you're still not convinced by this, it might bolster your confidence to recognize some of the vocabulary of the really rich, trigger words in an international lifestyle: Lamborghini's a car, Riva a boat; Christofle makes cutlery, Wedgwood or Sèvres your china, and glass is Baccarat or Lalique (not modern Cristal Lalique). Your stationery comes from Pineider or Smythsons, your beach towels from Hermès. There are lots of jewellers to choose from: Fred, Cartier (not Le Must), Bulgari, Van Cleef and Arpels, Harry Winston, Gerard...

If these aren't luxurious enough for you, here are some things that are really expensive to maintain: yacht, swimming pool, race horses and polo ponies, aeroplane or helicopter, Rolls Royce Phantom VI, furs, long fingernails, everything cashmere, pets and children, second homes. (A friend has a villa in the South of France; the washing machine went wrong while guests were staying there, so they phoned his office in London. Phone calls flew back and forth, between the villa and London, between London and the villa's caretaker in a nearby village – he went to try and fix the machine, couldn't... Many phone calls later it was discovered that all that was needed was a new washer, but the telephone bill was several hundred pounds.)

The top places to shop are Rodeo Drive (Los Angeles), Faubourg St Honoré (Paris), Bond Street (London), Via Veneto (Rome), Trump Tower (New York). Or if it's people you're after, try staying at the Palace (St Moritz and Lausanne), Ritz (London and Paris), Cipriani (Venice), or visiting nightclubs: Castel's in Paris, Annabel's in London, Palladium in New York (not London!)

You'll need the best bank account for all this. The best banks are

Swiss, followed by those in Lichtenstein; nearer home, Coutts, the Channel Islands and the Isle of Man. All money talks in America, but Manufacturers Hanover Trust has the edge; you have to be educated to be able to say it.

Finally, to speak this new-found vocabulary your accent should be Cockney, *real* Sloane (her), public school (him); real Boston, Memphis; French (her), Italian (him), Russian or Chinese. (Don't try learning these last two languages; there's a new alphabet to conquer first.)

Like all lists of essentials, these are just to get you by; you'll need to pick up lots more. Alternatively, you may carry on thinking rich knowing none of them.

Disclaimer

The author did not promise that this book would:

1   make you richer instantly
2   make you instantly more beautiful
3   make you more loved
4   make you smile
5   make you think

The author is being perfectly honest!

IT'S ALL UP

TO

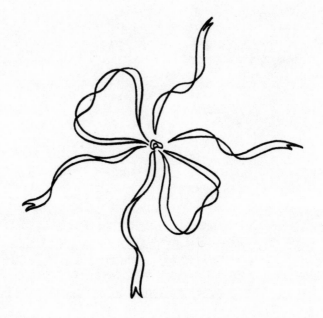

The richest thing about my life is the variety. No two days are alike. Let me tell you about yesterday. It was fun-filled, with not a minute free all day long. There were fittings in the shop all morning with amusing clients (one of the funniest men in Britain came with his girlfriend); a meeting with the curator of Stoke Museum about an exhibition of the history of hats where mine represent their evolution over the past decade; a drinks party at lunchtime at which I met a man who makes soap, the general who runs the Tower of London and Their Excellencies the Egyptian and Chinese ambassadors. Back at the shop in the afternoon, there was a duchess, a countess and later a bridal veil fitting. Then in the evening a super party: good dinner with smashing friends and stars, and Gloria Gaynor sang not just one but two of my favourite songs: 'I am what I am' and 'I will survive'.

Only that morning my Coutts Gold Card had arrived; surely an aid to thinking rich and getting broke?

The next day I looked at my diary and felt really rich – just a photo session in the morning and then a chance to finish this book. I couldn't help remembering sitting on a bed with Denis Quilley, Nikolas Grace and, best of all, Marie Helvin, and Marie confessing how hard she'd found writing *Catwalk*. If I'm honest, I have to admit that I've enjoyed writing every word of this, even doing it all in longhand. In fact, I've enjoyed it so much that it could become habit-forming: I can't wait to write another one, so don't think of this as the end but merely the interval (though I hope there might be some bits you'd like to go back to). In the meantime, if you still aren't yet thinking rich enough, may I suggest you just have to look at my photograph on the cover and tell yourself, 'If he can do it, anyone can – and so shall I!'

Till then, cheerio, à bientôt, ciao, shalom, adios.

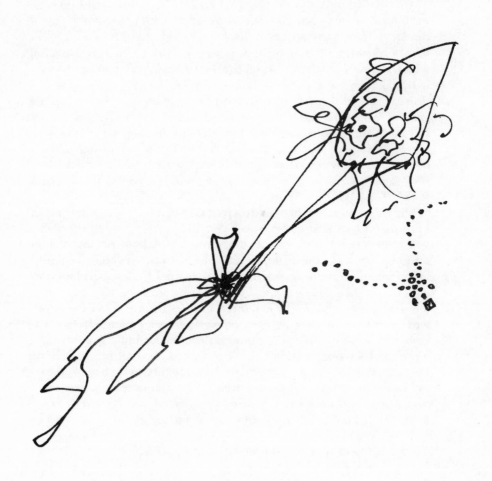

Acknowledgements

My thanks to all the following who have helped me: Agneta, Walter Annenberg, Lady Elizabeth Anson, Brigitta Appleby; Jacques Babando, Pattie Barron, Shirley Bassey, Jens Birger-Christensen, Cindy and Lenny Bitterman, Marc Bohan, Sir Arthur Bryan, Mark and Jane Burns; Simon Callow, Chris and Angharad Cazenove, Caroline Cheshire, Harry Cipriani, John Cox; Judith Dagworthy, Peter Daly, Roger and Heather Daltrey, Gillian and Caridig Davis, Anne Davison, Nancy Delman, Leslie-Ann Down, Lord and Lady Dunleath; Liz and David Emanuel, Audrey Eyton; Naomi and Jack Felber, Susan Farmer, Cosima Fry; Princess George Galitzine, Annemie Gilbert, Anne and Duncan Goodhew, Sue and John Green, Lloyd and Debbie Grossman; Marie Helvin, Annabel Heseltine, Chrissie Hinde, Min Hogg, David Hockney, Alistair Hughes; Rikki Jacquot; Paul and Fiona Jones; Tessa Dahl-Kelly, Soraya Khashoggi; Roger Lamb, Maureen Lipman (it was at her party that my Publishers discovered me), Joanna Lumley; The Earl and Countess of March, Laura, Duchess of Marlborough, Prince and Princess Stefano Massimo, Homayoun Masandi, Valerie Mendes; Nicky Haslam; Ian Ogilvy, James Ogilvy; Elaine Paige, Molly Parkin, The Hon. Mrs. Patrick Penny, Joanna Percy, Lady Philippa Phillips, Sian Phillips, Dominic Prince, Patrick Procktor; Katie Rabbett, Susan Rea (my extraordinarily patient Editor who learnt to decipher my writing! Thank you), Janet Reger, Marion Richardson, Cheryll Roberts, Viscountess Rothermere, Baron Phillipe Rothschild, The Hon. Henrietta Rous, Patrick and Marsha Ryecart; Lt-Cdr and Mrs Harold Shilling, Gertrude and Ronald Shilling, Lord and Lady Settrington, Roy Stephens, The Earl and Countess of Strafford, Anthony Swann; Jack Tinker, Caroline Treffgarne, Judith Turner, Thompson Twins; Roy Wadland, Dr Kurt and Kathy Wagner, Mrs Ward, Racquel Welch, Lucy Williams, David Wilson; The Marquess and Marchioness of Zetland... And as I'm bound to have missed out someone terribly important, may I take this opportunity to thank you too! (Well, at least you bought the book – didn't you?)

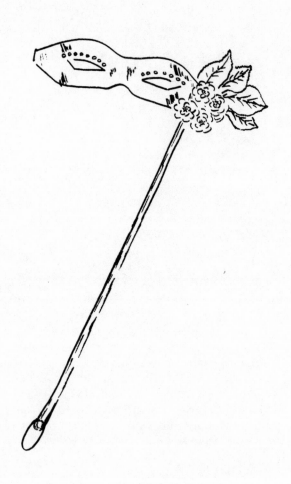

奇妙的瓷像世界

我們一向認為帽子是用來戴在頭上的，但是英國設計師大衞雪鈴（David Shilling）所設計的帽子卻並非這般簡單。

雪鈴的確設計過一些戴在頭上的帽子。自十二歲起，他便為母親設計華麗的帽子來參加著名的雅士閣賽馬，後來更成為著名的女帽設計師。他給帽子來一次革新，將它再次帶回時裝主流。由於雪鈴的設計極富藝術價值，所以被視為藝術品，部分更被放到紐約城市藝術博物館、倫敦維多利亞和愛爾拔博物館等地方作永久展覽。

一些時尚女士都愛將收集得來的雪鈴帽子放在客廳或畫室作裝飾，但真正瘋狂的收藏者實在需要一個櫃來儲存。不過，自數年前起，收藏家可用另一種方式來收藏帽子——收藏頭戴雪鈴帽子的精細骨瓷像。帽上的每朵花均由人手雕出及上色。

首批「雅士閣仕女」（Ascot Lady）瓷像為數甚少，卻象徵著一位知名時裝設計師與自十八世紀中葉起以精細瓷器馳名的高博公司（Coalport）合作的開始。